JAMES WELDON
JOHNSON

JAMES WELDON JOHNSON

Jane Tolbert-Rouchaleau

Senior Consulting Editor
Nathan Irvin Huggins
Director
W.E.B. Du Bois Institute for Afro-American Research
Harvard University

CHELSEA HOUSE PUBLISHERS
New York   New Haven   Philadelphia

Editor-in-Chief   Nancy Toff

Executive Editor   Remmel T. Nunn

Managing Editor   Karyn Gullen Browne

Copy Chief   Juliann Barbato

Picture Editor   Adrian G. Allen

Art Director   Giannella Garrett

Manufacturing Manager   Gerald Levine

Staff for JAMES WELDON JOHNSON

Senior Editor   Richard Rennert

Associate Editor   Perry King

Assistant Editor   Gillian Bucky

Copy Editor   James Guiry

Deputy Copy Chief   Ellen Scordato

Editorial Assistant   Susan DeRosa

Associate Picture Editor   Juliette Dickstein

Picture Researcher   Justine Blau

Senior Designer   Laurie Jewell

Design Assistant   Laura Lang

Production Coordinator   Joseph Romano

Cover Illustration   Alan J. Nahigian

Creative Director   Harold Steinberg

3   5   7   9   8   6   4   2

Library of Congress Cataloging in Publication Data

Tolbert-Rochaleau, Jane.
   James Weldon Johnson.

   (Black Americans of achievement)
   Bibliography: p.
   Includes index.
   1. Johnson, James Weldon, 1871–1938—Biography—Juvenile literature.   2. Authors, American—20th century—Biography—Juvenile literature.   3. Civil rights workers—United States—Biography—Juvenile literature. [1. Johnson, James Weldon, 1871–1938.   2. Authors, American.
3. Afro-Americans—Biography]
I. Title.   II. Series.
PS3519.O2625Z894   1988   818'.5209 [B] [92]   87-30012
ISBN 1-55546-596-X

We gratefully acknowledge the assistance given to us by Dr. Sandra Wilson of the Johnson Memorial Foundation in the preparation of this work.
Acknowledgment is also made to the Edward B. Marks Music Company for permission to reprint "Lift Every Voice and Sing" by Rosamond and James Weldon Johnson.

CONTENTS

BLACK
AMERICANS
OF
ACHIEVEMENT

MUHAMMAD ALI
heavyweight champion

RICHARD ALLEN
*founder of the
African Methodist
Episcopal church*

LOUIS ARMSTRONG
musician

JAMES BALDWIN
author

BENJAMIN BANNEKER
*scientist and
mathematician*

MARY MCLEOD BETHUNE
educator

BLANCHE K. BRUCE
politician

RALPH BUNCHE
diplomat

GEORGE WASHINGTON CARVER
botanist

CHARLES WADDELL CHESTNUTT
author

PAUL CUFFE
abolitionist

FREDERICK DOUGLASS
abolitionist editor

CHARLES R. DREW
physician

W. E. B. DUBOIS
educator and author

PAUL LAURENCE DUNBAR
poet

DUKE ELLINGTON
bandleader and composer

RALPH ELLISON
author

ELLA FITZGERALD
singer

MARCUS GARVEY
black-nationalist leader

PRINCE HALL
social reformer

WILLIAM H. HASTIE
educator and politician

MATTHEW A. HENSON
explorer

CHESTER HIMES
author

BILLIE HOLIDAY
singer

JOHN HOPE
educator

LENA HORNE
entertainer

LANGSTON HUGHES
poet

JAMES WELDON JOHNSON
author

SCOTT JOPLIN
composer

MARTIN LUTHER KING, JR.
civil rights leader

JOE LOUIS
heavyweight champion

MALCOLM X
militant black leader

THURGOOD MARSHALL
Supreme Court justice

ELIJAH MUHAMMAD
religious leader

JESSE OWENS
champion athlete

GORDON PARKS
photographer

SIDNEY POITIER
actor

ADAM CLAYTON POWELL, JR.
political leader

A. PHILIP RANDOLPH
labor leader

PAUL ROBESON
singer and actor

JACKIE ROBINSON
baseball great

JOHN RUSSWURM
publisher

SOJOURNER TRUTH
antislavery activist

HARRIET TUBMAN
antislavery activist

NAT TURNER
slave revolt leader

DENMARK VESEY
slave revolt leader

MADAME C. J. WALKER
entrepreneur

BOOKER T. WASHINGTON
educator

WALTER WHITE
political activist

RICHARD WRIGHT
author

ON
ACHIEVEMENT

— ❧ —

Coretta Scott King

BEFORE YOU BEGIN this book, I hope you will ask yourself
what the word excellence means to you. I think that it's a question we
should all ask, and keep asking as we grow older and change. Because the
truest answer to it should never change. When you think of excellence,
perhaps you think of success at work; or of becoming wealthy; or meeting
the right person, getting married, and having a good family life.

Those important goals are worth striving for, but there is a better way
to look at excellence. As Martin Luther King, Jr., said in one of his last
sermons, "I want you to be first in love. I want you to be first in moral
excellence. I want you to be first in generosity. If you want to be
important, wonderful. If you want to be great, wonderful. But recognize
that he who is greatest among you shall be your servant."

My husband, Martin Luther King, Jr., knew that the true meaning of
achievement is service. When I met him, in 1952, he was already
ordained as a Baptist preacher and was working towards a doctoral degree
at Boston University. I was studying at the New England Conservatory
and dreamed of accomplishments in music. We married a year later, and
after I graduated the following year we moved to Montgomery, Alabama.
We didn't know it then, but our notions of achievement were about to
undergo a dramatic change.

You may have read or heard about what happened next. What began
with the boycott of a local bus line grew into a national movement, and
by the time he was assassinated in 1968 my husband had fashioned a
black movement powerful enough to shatter forever the practice of racial
segregation. What you may not have read about is where he got his
method for resisting injustice without compromising his religious beliefs.

He got the strategy of nonviolence from a man of a different race, who lived in a distant country, and even practiced a different religion. The man was Mahatma Gandhi, the great leader of India, who devoted his life to serving humanity in the spirit of love and nonviolence. It was in these principles that Martin discovered his method for social reform. More than anything else, those two principles were the key to his achievements.

This book is about black Americans who served society through the excellence of their achievements. It forms a part of the rich history of black men and women in America—a history of stunning accomplishments in every field of human endeavor, from literature and art to science, industry, education, diplomacy, athletics, jurisprudence, even polar exploration.

Not all of the people in this history had the same ideals, but I think you will find something that all of them have in common. Like Martin Luther King, Jr., they all decided to become "drum majors" and serve humanity. In that principle—whether it was expressed in books, inventions, or song—they found something outside themselves to use as a goal and a guide. Something that showed them a way to serve others, instead of living only for themselves.

Reading the stories of these courageous men and women not only helps us discover the principles that we will use to guide our own lives, but it teaches us about our black heritage and about America itself. It is crucial for us to know the heroes and heroines of our history and to realize that the price we paid in our struggle for equality in America was dear. But we must also understand that we have gotten as far as we have partly because America's democratic system and ideals made it possible.

We still are struggling with racism and prejudice. But the great men and women in this series are a tribute to the spirit of our democratic ideals and the system in which they have flourished. And that makes their stories special, and worth knowing. ◖◗

JAMES WELDON
JOHNSON

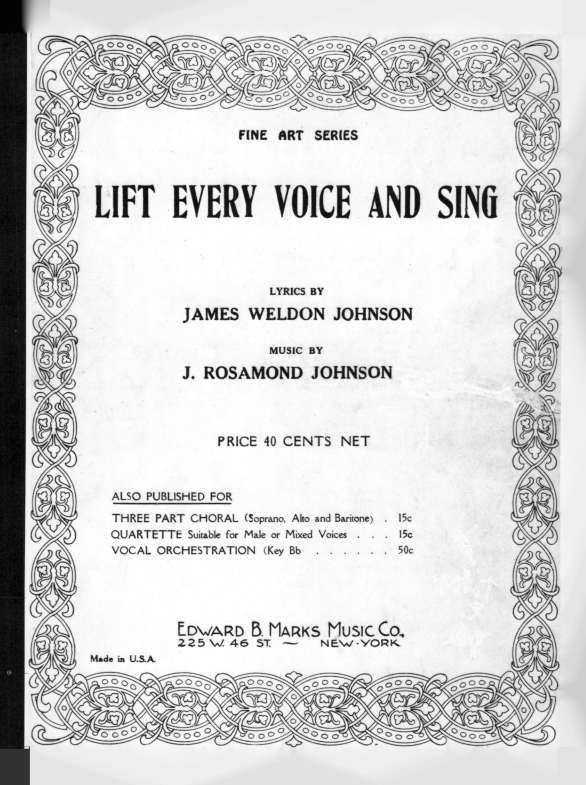

1

LIFT EVERY
VOICE

ON AN AFTERNOON in early February 1900, James Weldon Johnson paced the front porch of his house in Jacksonville, Florida, continually repeating the verses to a song he had just finished composing. The 28-year-old principal of an all-black public school in Jacksonville had written the song, entitled "Lift Every Voice and Sing," to celebrate the 91st anniversary of the birth of President Abraham Lincoln. His students were going to be singing it at an upcoming town ceremony honoring Lincoln, whose signing of the Emancipation Proclamation had freed millions of slaves in the South during the Civil War.

Tall, slender, and mustachioed, Johnson started to recite once more the words that he had composed in his head. The first verse began:

> Lift every voice and sing
> Till earth and heaven ring
> Ring with the harmonies of Liberty

As Johnson paced on the porch, his brother, Rosamond, was inside the house finishing the music that would accompany the lyrics. Rosamond was a professional musician, and he had composed a stirring, upbeat melody to match the buoyant nature of his brother's verses. Johnson had wanted the song to recapture the spirit of hope and rejoicing that all black

"Lift Every Voice and Sing" was written by Johnson and his brother, Rosamond, in 1900. The stirring song later became known as the black national anthem.

11

Johnson was working as a school principal when he wrote the lyrics to "Lift Every Voice and Sing." The song is noted for calling forth the pride that blacks have in their heritage and for expressing their hopes for a better future.

Americans and every opponent of slavery had felt on January 1, 1863, when the Emancipation Proclamation had been enacted.

> Stony the road we trod
> Bitter the chastening rod,
> Felt in the days when hope unborn died

The words spoke of the harsh conditions endured by blacks on their road from slavery. Their hopes for freedom and justice had not died; some had been given life over a period of time, prompting Johnson to write:

> Out from the gloomy past,
> Till now we stand at last
> Where the white gleam of our bright star is cast.

Johnson refused to be pessimistic about the future of blacks even though discriminatory laws passed in the previous two decades had robbed them of many of the advances they had made in the era immediately following the Civil War. If slavery had been brought to an end, then racial inequality could also be stopped. But it would require men of principle to stand up and take action, as Lincoln had done in 1863.

Moved by feelings of both anguish and joy, Johnson could not keep from crying as he repeated yet another passage:

> God of our weary years,
> God of our silent tears,
> Thou who has brought us thus far on the way;

The lyrics hearkened back to the powerful black spirituals that slaves once sang to give themselves strength as they labored in the fields. Religious faith still continued to play a strong role in the struggle for civil rights.

Johnson's younger brother, Rosamond (shown here), was an accomplished musician and composer. The two brothers became part of one of America's best-known songwriting teams in the early 1900s.

"Lift Every Voice and Sing" was written to help celebrate the anniversary of Abraham Lincoln's birth. Because the president signed the Emancipation Proclamation, he came to be regarded as a savior by many black Americans.

Johnson then spoke the final three lines of his song:

> May we forever stand.
> True to our God,
> True to our native land.

These lines addressed the need for Americans to remain loyal to their country in spite of all its imperfections. Lincoln had fought to unite the nation after it had been torn apart by disagreements between the North and the South. Johnson felt that black and white Americans must continue the struggle to ensure that *all* citizens were given the rights guaranteed to them by the Constitution.

After making a few final revisions to the song, the Johnson brothers decided it was ready to be sung in public. On February 12, 1900, the Stanton School chorus performed "Lift Every Voice and Sing" during the town's celebration of Lincoln's birthday. The song was met with a very warm reception, but in the years that followed, the two brothers became so involved in their careers that they did not give much more thought to it.

Nevertheless, "Lift Every Voice and Sing" was not forgotten. Copies of the song slowly began to circulate—until Johnson's message of hope and pride was eventually taken to heart by black organizations throughout the country, and the song unofficially became known as the black national anthem. The lyrics inspired generations to dream of a time when blacks and whites could sit down together in friendship and understanding and be treated as equal citizens. People of all different races found encouragement in these lyrics and lifted their voices to echo the sentiments expressed in the anthem. As Johnson later admitted, "We wrote better than we knew."

Sing a song full of the faith that the dark past has taught us.
Sing a song full of the hope that the present has brought us.

While Johnson was writing this song at the turn of the century, he knew that the ultimate triumph of liberty and justice over racial oppression was a long way off. However, in his life's work as well as in this song, he insisted on looking forward to a time when blacks would have a more prominent place in American society.

No matter whether Johnson was employed as a songwriter, poet, novelist, diplomat, journalist, or civil rights leader, he always worked hard to help others envision a time of promise, encouraging them to press their demands for racial equality. "Lift Every Voice and Sing" was written while he was in the midst of the first of several careers, and it was only one of many steps taken by him in his march toward a new era of civil rights for all black Americans.

2

HIGHER
LEARNING

◦◦◦◦

J AMES WELDON JOHNSON was born in Jacksonville, Florida, on June 17, 1871. He was the eldest surviving child of James and Helen Dillet Johnson.

The strong intellectual interests and leadership qualities that James displayed as he grew up were heavily influenced by his parents. His father was born free of slavery in Richmond, Virginia, in 1830. As a young man, James's father moved to New York, where he worked as a waiter and eventually gained the respectable position of headwaiter in a hotel dining room.

James's mother was a woman of mixed black and French descent. She was the daughter of the postmaster of Nassau, the largest city in the British-ruled chain of West Indian islands known as the Bahamas. Black Bahamians had been given their freedom in the 1830s when Great Britain abolished slavery in all parts of its empire.

Helen Dillet was educated in New York, where she met her future husband. She and her family returned to Nassau at the outbreak of the Civil War because they feared that free blacks in the North would be enslaved if the South won the war. The senior James Johnson followed her to Nassau, where

The son of educated, well-to-do parents, Johnson was born and raised in Jacksonville, Florida, where his father was the headwaiter at the fancy St. James Hotel (shown here).

James Johnson, Sr. (shown here in the uniform of the Mason society), worked as a waiter in New York City and in the Bahamas before settling in the fast-growing, Florida resort town of Jacksonville.

he became a headwaiter for the grand Royal Victoria Hotel. The two were married in 1864.

Life in the Bahamas was relatively free of racial prejudice. During the Civil War, the islands prospered as ports for fast merchant ships running the Union blockades to supply the South. But the end of the Civil War in 1865, coupled with a devastating hurricane the next year, virtually destroyed the island economy. Learning from guests at the hotel that Florida was becoming a popular tourist area, the senior James Johnson moved his wife and recently born daughter to Jacksonville, which was quickly becoming a prosperous winter resort for rich northerners.

Jacksonville was a growing but still largely undeveloped town when the Johnsons moved there in 1869. Helen Dillet Johnson missed the cultural activities of New York and the old colonial elegance of Nassau. But the senior James Johnson was determined to make a home for himself and his family in a place where they could find opportunities to advance. Blacks made up more than half of Jacksonville's population; they had taken advantage of their newly won right to vote and had assumed many political positions in the town government. These steps were possible because Union troops stationed throughout the South helped to protect the rights of blacks. During the Reconstruction era, which lasted from 1867 to 1877, many blacks also won election to state legislatures.

Soon after arriving in Jacksonville, the senior James Johnson took a job as a headwaiter in a local hotel and bought a small, dilapidated house in a new, mainly lower-class white section of Jacksonville. Helen's parents joined them at the house, but soon after they came, the Johnsons' infant daughter died. A year later, James Weldon Johnson was born. His brother, John Rosamond Johnson, who was known by his middle name, was born in 1873. At that time, the Johnsons also adopted a teenage girl, Agnes Edwards.

During the time that James was growing up, Florida's economy was booming. New railroads were built to reach the orange groves and the tourist resorts that were springing up all over the state. The Johnsons also prospered. Soon after James's birth, his father built a larger house on their plot of land. To young James, the house seemed like a mansion, and it was at least as fine as the homes of his white neighbors.

In 1864, Helen Dillet married James Johnson, Sr., while he was working at the Royal Victoria Hotel (shown here) in Nassau, the capital of the Bahamas.

The racial climate in Jacksonville was more tolerant than in most of the other towns in the United States. Although segregation was enforced in the school system and blacks maintained their own separate churches, the black community was very active in civic affairs and owned many of the town's thriving businesses. In many areas of the South, there were no schools at all for black children. Jacksonville's all-

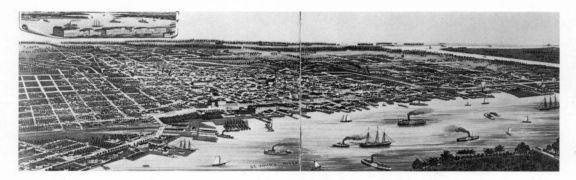

Steamships crowd the St. John's River in this illustration of Jacksonville, Florida. Johnson's hometown had a reputation as a good town for black residents in the late 1800s.

black Stanton School offered its students an education up to the eighth grade and was considered to be one of the best black primary schools in the country.

James grew up in a stimulating educational environment. His father, a self-taught man, met many influential people at the hotel where he worked and was a friend of some of the country's leading black citizens. James's mother was a teacher at the Stanton School and had a strong hand in her sons' education. Helen and the senior James Johnson instilled in their sons a strong belief in academic achievement and in maintaining high personal standards. They also made their sons aware of their obligation to help people who were less fortunate than themselves.

The Johnson house was filled with books, and James became an avid reader. He enjoyed reading from the family's large illustrated Bible, and he also read popular American writers and poets as well as works by the English novelist Charles Dickens. Music, too, was important in the Johnson household; James and his brother were taught how to play the piano and guitar by their mother. James practiced dutifully and learned how to read music, although it was Rosamond who really seemed to excel in music.

A studious, well-behaved boy, James also loved playing marbles and baseball with the neighborhood children. His early ambition to be a drummer in a marching band later turned to desires to be a journalist, doctor, and lawyer. These goals were encouraged by his parents, who urged him to set sights for himself that were far higher than those of most other black children of his time.

James's horizons were widened by visits to New York City during summer breaks in the mid-1880s to visit his mother's relatives. Accompanied on these trips by his grandmother, James learned about life in the big city while playing in the streets of the borough of Brooklyn with children of many different racial and ethnic backgrounds. The visits to New York introduced him to the excitement of an urban environment and gave him a glimpse of the cultural life that a big city could offer.

James's grandmother was a strong-minded, religious woman, and she exerted a great deal of influence over him. She hoped that James would become an evangelical preacher when he grew up, and she took him to church meetings where he heard black spirituals sung and where the congregation engaged in dances, chants, and exercises of religious frenzy. Although James's parents were devoted members of the

Johnson (front row, far right) poses with his fellow students at the Stanton School. Raised in a household filled with books, he was always a good student.

As a youth, Johnson went to hear the distinguished orator and civil rights leader Frederick Douglass (shown here) give a speech in Jacksonville. Johnson was deeply impressed by the man whose autobiography he had won in a school contest. He maintained, "No one could ever forget a first sight of Frederick Douglass."

local Ebenezer Methodist Episcopal Church (James's father later became a minister) they were not enthusiastic about the more folk-oriented type of religious meetings that Grandmother Dillet preferred. As James grew older, he began to feel that many of the practices of his grandmother's congregation were a bit out of the ordinary. His doubts about his religious faith would increase over time, yet he greatly valued his childhood exposure to the impassioned sermons of traveling preachers and to spirituals, which he called the black people's "most treasured heritage."

Among James's childhood friends was Ricardo Ponce, a Cuban boy of mixed ancestry, who stayed with the Johnsons for a while when James was a teenager. Ricardo taught James and Rosamond how to speak Spanish. Another of James's friends was Judson Wetmore, a light-skinned black from Jacksonville whose features allowed him to pass for white. His ability to move within both the black and white societies fascinated James.

When James was a teenager, he worked for the local newspaper, the Florida *Times-Union*, during after-school hours. Starting as a mail room assistant and then working as an office boy for the editor-in-chief, he learned how a newspaper is published and began to have ambitions of being a journalist. He also played for the baseball team of Jacksonville's leading black social club and was well known for his tricky curveball.

James's education at Jacksonville's Stanton School ended when he graduated from the eighth grade in 1887. Stanton had been started shortly after the Civil War by the Freedmen's Bureau, a federal organization that had been formed to administer to the needs of former slaves. At this school, James's mother had become the first black female public school teacher in Florida.

Stanton's program gave James a thorough grounding in reading, writing, and arithmetic—the subjects that formed the basis of the educational curriculums at other American public schools. Discipline was strictly enforced at Stanton, and the school's administrators were determined that its graduates should be outstanding representatives of the black community. However, few students remained at the school through the eighth (and final) grade. When James graduated at the age of 16, he was one of an elite group of educated black students.

After James graduated from eighth grade, his parents had to decide where to send him to continue his education. The local high school only accepted white students. However, Howard University and a number of other all-black educational institutions had recently been established in the South to give black students a chance for secondary schooling. James's parents debated over where to send him and finally chose the Preparatory Division of Atlanta University in Georgia, the closest of the best black schools. The institution's goal was to prepare young men and women for teaching positions and jobs in other professions. Although the school was chiefly known for its university, Atlanta University also had a separate program for high school students.

When James took a train to Atlanta in 1887, he was accompanied by his friends Ricardo Ponce and Judson Wetmore, who had also enrolled at the university. All three planned to take two years of preparatory courses before entering the college program. Arriving at the school, they found three ivy-covered buildings located on the grounds of a former Confederate fort. Most of their classmates were the sons and daughters of the best black families in Georgia.

The school, which had been started by a church organization in 1869 and whose administration and faculty were white, emphasized a liberal arts education. Its older students were given courses in Greek

When he was a teenager, Johnson took a job with a local newspaper. He said, "I gradually became possessed with the idea that I should like to run a newspaper—to edit it—to write."

and Latin, literature, philosophy, rhetoric, mathematics, and science. Industrial arts courses such as carpentry and mechanical drafting were also taught. Although black studies were not part of the curriculum, racial topics were often the subjects of the school's public-speaking contests.

The students' time outside the classroom was closely regulated. Study and prayer occupied much of their day. Males and females were taught in separate classes and were kept apart on the campus to maintain their high moral conduct.

The strict code of conduct enforced by the university was designed to produce students with strong moral characters. The university officials believed that well-educated, upstanding students would best be able to deal with the racial discrimination and segregation that they would face throughout their lives. Many of the students consequently left Atlanta University with a strong sense of duty to their race.

During the six years that Johnson spent at Atlanta University, the cost for a year's tuition and room and board was about $100. Stone Hall, one of the school's main buildings, is shown here.

James thrived at the school. His classmates respected his talents as a baseball player and liked to hear his stories about his trips to New York City. He also wrote poetry, and some of his love poems soon earned him a reputation as a ladies' man. He was amazed by the power that a well-written verse could have over a reader. Consequently, he began to write in different styles of poetry.

When James returned to Jacksonville after his first year at the university, he was looking forward to seeing his family again. Rosamond, who had become active in musical and literary groups, introduced James to the new black cultural societies that had recently been started. However, soon after James returned home, his mother began to suffer from a crippling case of rheumatism. Although she tried to remain cheerful, it was deeply distressing to James to see his 46-year-old mother struggling to walk.

That same summer, a yellow fever epidemic spread through Jacksonville, and a quarantine was enforced on town residents for a couple of months. Because James could not return to Atlanta, his father hired a tutor: a shoemaker from the West Indies who turned out to be a true scholar with a vast knowledge of drama, poetry, and classical works. The lessons ranged over a number of subjects and included discussions about Julius Caesar's *Gallic Wars*, which describes some of the history and politics of ancient Rome.

When it became clear that the quarantine would force James to miss the full year at Atlanta University, he decided to look for a job. He was surprised when he was hired by Thomas Summers, a well-known Jacksonville surgeon who needed an assistant who could read Latin. Summers, who was white, treated his young receptionist as a colleague. They also shared literary interests; Summers was a published poet, and he provided James with encouragement and criticism for the poems he had written at the university. James

Johnson with his brother, Rosamond (center), and friend Ricardo Ponce (right). While Rosamond studied music at the New England Conservatory, Johnson and the Cuban-born Ponce enrolled at Atlanta University.

greatly admired Summers and tried to model himself after the urbane, cultured doctor. He also began to study medicine and anatomy so that he could become a surgeon.

James returned to Atlanta University in the fall of 1889 and continued to work on his poetry. Most of his poems dealt with friendship, love, and death, and some were published in the school newspaper, on which he worked. Besides writing poetry, he also became one of the lead singers in the university glee club.

In 1891, at the end of his freshman year at Atlanta University, James took a summer teaching job in Henry County in rural Georgia. For the first time, he came into contact with the living conditions of the impoverished black farmers of the South. His pay was based on student attendance, so he traveled around to the tenant farmers, trying to convince them to send their children to the shack where his classes were held. He was successful in his efforts, and with the few books available he was able to help some of the children learn the alphabet.

James returned to Henry County to teach during the summer of 1892. During his time in the country, he lived with local farm families and enjoyed spending time with his pleasant, hardworking hosts. Life in the country ultimately prompted him to incorporate the informal southern black dialect that he heard into his poetry.

Although James's cultural and educational background differed from that of the rural people, he shared a common bond of race. As he wrote later, "They were me, and I was they; that a force stronger than blood made us one." He believed that the black farmers' love of laughter and song in the face of their oppressive conditions was truly admirable. He began to discover the beauty of the entire black race, and he also awoke to his mission of helping his fellowman achieve racial equality.

After James entered the college-level program at Atlanta University, he began to work on his public-speaking skills, which he had previously considered to be one of his weaknesses. In 1892, he won the school's oratory contest with a speech that discussed methods for reducing racial discrimination. Maintaining that blacks were not treated according to individual merit but rather as a group, he stated that blacks must learn middle-class values and seize educational opportunities in order to change white attitudes toward blacks.

During James's college years, discriminatory measures known as Jim Crow laws were being passed by the southern states. The new laws reversed the civil rights acts that had been enacted after the Civil War and legalized segregation. Riding the train between Jacksonville and Atlanta, James continually ran up against Jim Crow rules that relegated blacks to racially segregated, second-class cars. On his first trip to Atlanta in 1887, he and Ricardo Ponce had been mistaken for foreigners when the train conductor heard

During Johnson's college years, he spent two summers in rural Georgia teaching the alphabet to the children of sharecroppers, who grew mostly cotton.

Poet Paul Laurence Dunbar (shown here) met Johnson in the summer of 1893, when both young men were working at the World's Columbian Exhibition in Chicago, Illinois. They soon became close friends.

them speaking Spanish. Because black foreigners at that time were not subjected to the Jim Crow laws, the two young men were allowed to stay in the first-class car, which was for whites only. But on another train ride, in the company of three Atlanta University students, James told the conductor that he and his friends were not going to give up their seats in the white car. When they were told that a white mob would be waiting for them at one of the train stops, they angrily moved.

During the summer of 1893, James led a contingent of Atlanta University students who traveled to the World's Columbian Exposition, an international fair in Chicago, Illinois. James and his friends found jobs as chairboys—guides who pushed visitors around in wheelchairs. Although the contributions of black Americans to their country were given little recognition at the fair, a Colored People's Day was ultimately scheduled. The main speaker, the renowed black antislavery and civil rights leader Frederick Douglass, made a blistering attack on racial discrimination and received a long ovation from the black crowd. At the fair, James befriended Paul Laurence Dunbar, a young poet serving as Douglass's assistant who would soon become well known for writing poems that featured black folk dialect.

James was graduated from Atlanta University in the spring of 1894 as the top student in his class. Because he had played a prominent role in the school's glee club, university officials asked him to be part of a singing group, the Atlanta University Quartet, that was going to make a fund-raising tour of New England towns, giving recitals of black spirituals. In this endeavor, the school was following the example of the Jubilee Singers of Fisk University in Nashville, Tennesee, who had performed spirituals while touring throughout the United States and Europe.

After the summer concert tour ended, James was

faced with a difficult choice. He was offered a chance to study medicine at Harvard University, but he was also asked by the Jacksonville school board to replace the principal of the Stanton School, who was retiring. Although he was tempted by the medical scholarship, he eventually decided that a career in education would best fulfill his desire to help his people. In the fall of 1894, he returned home.

Johnson (at far right) toured New England as part of the Atlanta University Quartet following his graduation from Atlanta University in 1894. He continued to pursue his interest in music some years later, when he embarked on a songwriting career.

UNDER THE BAMBOO TREE

BY COLE AND JOHNSON BROS

A SUCCESSFUL INTERPOLATION BY MARIE CAHILL IN SALLY IN OUR ALLEY

HOUSE HITS

Published by JOS. W. STERN & CO. 34 East 21st St. NEW YORK
MARKSTERN BUILDING

NEW YORK
CHICAGO
LONDON

LONDON JOS. W. STERN & CO.

3

BACK
TO SCHOOL

W HEN JOHNSON BECAME principal of the
Stanton School in 1894, he was faced with a huge
assignment. The 23-year-old college graduate was the
head of one of the largest public schools in Florida
and was in charge of 25 teachers (one of whom was
his adoptive sister, Agnes Edwards) and more than
1,000 students. His mother, who had been an assistant principal at the school, had retired in 1888
after her rheumatism incapacitated her. Johnson tended
to her in his parents' house (he would continue to
stay there during the years that he remained in Jacksonville).

Although Johnson was glad for the challenge that
came with being a principal, he had some doubts
about his ability to do the job. He wrote:

> Can I actually do it? . . . My position is an important
> one. Relatively, it is far more important than the prin-
> cipalship of the white grammar school. . . . I shall be
> scrutinized. I shall meet with envy and antagonism on
> the outside; and, perhaps, with disloyalty on the inside.

*Although Johnson originally in-
tended to pursue a career in education, by 1900 he had set his
sights on winning fame and fortune in the entertainment world.
"Under the Bamboo Tree" was
one of the first big hits that he
helped to produce as part of Cole
and the Johnson Brothers songwriting team.*

Even though Johnson was the principal of a large
and important school, he could not associate with
white colleagues at white public schools without
arousing racial antagonism. In 1894, he visited Central Grammar School, a local white school, so that
he could compare teaching methods and observe
classes. However, the parents of the white students

As the Stanton School's principal, Johnson (at far right) extended the school's curriculum by two grades so that students could be taught algebra, physics, and other advanced courses. He is shown here with one of his graduating classes.

reacted angrily to the appearance of a black man in the classes and filed complaints with the Jacksonville School Board. Although the administrators of Central Grammar School spoke out strongly in defense of Johnson, he was deeply disappointed by the uproar that his visit had caused.

Johnson went about his duties as principal with his customary dedication and enthusiasm. At the end of his first year as principal, 26 students were graduated from the eighth grade. Johnson convinced some of the graduates to remain for another year of schooling. The following year, he extended the school curriculum to include a 10th grade. He taught the courses in the two new grades himself, giving the advanced students instruction in such subjects as algebra, basic physics, and Spanish.

Out of a sense of mission to his race, Johnson began publishing a daily newspaper, the *Daily American*, in May 1895. The newspaper did more than provide Jacksonville's black community with a voice and local news; it enabled Johnson to become a spokesman for his people. His friend Judson Wetmore worked as a reporter, and other friends loaned him money to finance the newspaper.

Johnson's editorials in the *Daily American* sought to dispel racial stereotypes and stressed the importance of civil rights and equal opportunity. He demanded that the white community treat blacks honorably: "Give him fair play, then let him survive or perish." However, Johnson was battling in an increasingly hostile racial climate; blacks had already lost many of the rights they had won during the Reconstruction era. A variety of discriminatory rules were being passed to prevent blacks from voting or from applying for jobs in their local governments. Clearly, blacks were being given neither fair play nor equal opportunity.

In some of Johnson's editorials, he condemned Florida state laws that penalized with fines or imprisonment the clergymen and other educators who conducted nonsegregated private schools. Johnson believed that the state had no right to force private organizations to accept segregation.

Despite Johnson's best efforts to win a large black readership, the *Daily American* soon ran into financial difficulties. His newspaper was unable to compete with the Florida *Times-Union* and other local newspapers. He printed his last issue of the paper in early 1896. The *Daily American* was published for only eight months.

Because being principal of the Stanton School did not use up all of Johnson's energy, he continued to write poetry in his spare time. In the fall of 1896, he embarked on still another career while maintaining his job at the school. For a few hours each day, he worked in the office of a white lawyer named Thomas Ledwith. At the same time, he began to study for the bar exam. He hoped that he would be better able to represent the black community as a lawyer.

During the time that Johnson had been attending Atlanta University, his younger brother, Rosamond,

While Johnson served as an administrator and teacher at the Stanton School, he still found the time to write poetry, pass the Florida bar exam, and begin a daily newspaper devoted to the interests of the black community.

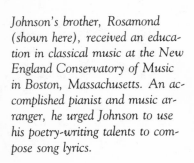

Johnson's brother, Rosamond (shown here), received an education in classical music at the New England Conservatory of Music in Boston, Massachusetts. An accomplished pianist and music arranger, he urged Johnson to use his poetry-writing talents to compose song lyrics.

had spent six years studying music at the New England Conservatory in Boston, Massachusetts. Rosamond published music and wrote librettos for operas. He then went on a national tour with *Oriental America*, a traveling show that performed a variety of popular black musical entertainments. In 1896, he returned to Jacksonville and found work as a music teacher. He also served as choir director and organist for a large Baptist church.

Johnson was intrigued by his brother's work. "His enthusiasm roused my curiosity about this new world into which he had a peep," Johnson wrote. He soon became aware of his own strong desire for the adventure that a musical career offered. After reading some of Johnson's poems, Rosamond decided that they would make wonderful lyrics to songs, and he composed melodies for a number of them.

Rosamond later wrote a light operatic piece for the Stanton School graduation ceremonies. At the commencement, the graduating students sang the operetta and performed a short dance at the conclusion of the piece. Johnson was criticized by Jacksonville's clergymen for introducing music and dance into the graduation ceremony; they claimed that the musically minded Johnson was "leading the children to the ballroom."

In 1897, Johnson passed his bar examination and was certified to practice law in the state of Florida. To gain his license, he had to endure a grueling, two-hour interrogation by a committee of three of the town's leading attorneys. One of the men was extremely hostile to blacks. When it became obvious during the examination that Johnson was qualified to practice law, the bigoted committee member stormed out of the room, yelling, "I'll be damned if I'll stay here to see him admitted." Johnson subsequently became the first black to be admitted to the bar in Duval County, an area that includes Jacksonville, and he was later admitted to the Florida Supreme Court.

Encouraged by Johnson's example, Judson Wetmore had also begun studying law. Wetmore passed the bar exam in 1898, and that summer he and Johnson opened a law office in Jacksonville. However, Johnson soon found that he was not interested in the paperwork and the more mundane details of his legal practice, and he left most of the work to Wetmore.

Instead of attending to his new practice, Johnson began working with his brother on a comic opera entitled *Tolosa, or the Royal Document*. The brothers set their opera on a Pacific island, and the story concerns Tolosa, daughter of the island king, who is in love with a commoner but who is also pursued by an unscrupulous American patent medicine salesman,

Composer Scott Joplin helped to popularize ragtime music, an art form that was mainly developed by blacks, in the early 1900s.

Dr. Hocus Pocus. The work was composed in the style of the comic operas written by the popular British composing team of William Gilbert and Arthur Sullivan.

The musical community of Jacksonville, of which Rosamond was a respected member, closely followed the development of the opera and offered encouragement. After it was completed, the owner of a major department store gave a party in honor of the Johnson brothers. Songs from *Tolosa* were played at the party, which was attended by black and white artists and prominent citizens. The comic opera was never actually produced, but it demonstrated that the Johnson brothers could write a long musical work.

A songwriter's success depended at that time on sales of the sheet music of his songs. Phonographs had not yet achieved wide distribution, so record sales did not amount to very much. Because most sheet music was sold for people to play on their pianos at home, a successful song had to have a fairly simple melody.

New York City was the music-publishing capital of America, and the district around Broadway and the streets in the West 40s—commonly known as Tin Pan Alley—was the center of a thriving entertainment industry. At the end of the school year, in June 1899, James and Rosamond Johnson left Jacksonville for New York.

The Johnsons came to New York equipped with samples of their work and an "invincible faith" in themselves. Johnson later wrote of his first attempt at a songwriting career, "I can now recognize all the absurdities and count up all the improbabilities." However, the Johnsons at the time were sure that their talent would allow them to establish themselves in the music business.

While in New York, the brothers rented rooms on West 53rd Street, near the center of the city's

music-publishing district. Johnson renewed his acquaintance with Paul Laurence Dunbar, the young poet whose dialect verses caught the spirit of black American life. Since their first meeting in 1893 in Chicago, Dunbar had become a well-established poet, and Johnson greatly admired his work. The Johnsons also met Oscar Hammerstein (the grandfather of the well-known composer of the same name), a manager of opera houses. He showed some interest in *Tolosa*, although he decided not to produce the opera.

The brothers also formed a friendship with a talented musician named Bob Cole, who directed and sang in a group called the Black Patti Troubadours. The three men teamed up to write a love song called "Louisiana Lize," which became their first success. The popular singer May Irwin bought the singing

Formed in 1900, Cole and the Johnson Brothers songwriting team was eventually credited with more than 200 successful songs. Johnson is shown here flanked by Bob Cole (left) and Rosamond.

BLACK PATTI *TROUBADOURS*

DIRECTION VOELKEL & NOLAN

THE BUCK-DANCING CONTEST

The Black Patti Troubadours were the most renowned black vaudeville group in America in the late 1800s. Bob Cole performed with the group before teaming with the Johnson Brothers.

rights to "Louisiana Lize," which was published by Joseph Stern and Company, a music firm that was known then as the House of Hits.

To Johnson, New York seemed to be "a new world—an alluring world, a tempting world, a world of greatly lessened restraints, a world of fascinating perils; but, above all, a world of tremendous artistic potentialities." Accordingly, he began to think deeply about black folk culture and the way that the themes and rhythms of black art and music could be used for his own work.

In the fall of 1900, the two brothers returned to Jacksonville, and Johnson resumed his duties at the Stanton School for the new school year. Influenced by Dunbar, he again began to write dialect poetry and produced "Sence You Went Away." Printed in *Century Magazine*, the poem became Johnson's first success with a major publication. "Sence You Went Away" was put to music by Rosamond, and it was later recorded by several major artists, including the internationally recognized singer and actor Paul Robeson. The lyrics begin:

Seems lak to me de stars don't shine so bright,
Seems lak to me de sun done loss his light,
Seems lak to me der's nothing goin' right,
Sence you went away.

Eager to try new musical arrangements on the Jacksonville community, the Johnsons staged a concert in early 1900 that featured original songs performed by Sidney Woodward, a professional singer from Boston, Massachusetts. The brothers also composed "Lift Every Voice and Sing," which was sung by 500 Jacksonville schoolchildren at a town celebration.

Johnson's attempt to juggle careers in education, law, and music pulled him in many directions. His law partner, Wetmore, was growing increasingly unhappy about Johnson's absences from the office. Their association soon came to an end.

Part of the reason for Johnson's disinterest in his law practice was that there were few opportunities for black lawyers at the time. Because of the high degree of racial prejudice in the court system, most blacks believed that it was advantageous to have a white lawyer represent them rather than a lawyer who was black.

In the summer of 1900—at the end of another school year—the Johnsons returned to New York and renewed their acquaintance with Bob Cole. The three men formed a songwriting partnership known as Cole and the Johnson Brothers. May Irwin asked them to write songs for a musical, *The Belle of Bridgeport*. Among their more popular songs for this show was "I Ain't Gwinter Work No Mo'."

Towering clouds of smoke rise over Jacksonville, Florida, as people flee with their possessions, seeking to escape the fire that destroyed two-thirds of the town in May 1901.

However, the Cole and Johnson Brothers partnership began at a grim time. That summer, racial tensions in New York boiled over one day after a white policeman was killed by a black. Mobs of whites roamed the streets and assaulted blacks. The Johnsons were not attacked, but some of their friends were badly injured. This race riot spurred a movement of blacks to a more isolated area in upper New York City known as Harlem.

The Johnson brothers returned home to Jacksonville in the fall of 1900 after having made some new inroads in the New York music establishment. The following spring, Dunbar visited the Johnsons for six weeks. He wrote a number of poems during his stay, and Rosamond set two of them to music—including one that would become a minor classic, "Li'l Gal."

In May 1901, a fire swept through Jacksonville, razing two-thirds of the town, including the Stanton School. The black section of town, which was left unprotected by the fire department, was especially hard hit. The Johnsons saved the school's records shortly before the building burned. Fortunately, their family home escaped the flames. It became a shelter for 25 of their friends.

Jacksonville's civil authorities set up temporary housing in the buildings that still stood. Companies of white militiamen were brought in to enforce martial law, but many of these troops provoked racial hostilities. In addition to these hostilities, Johnson observed a photographer paying blacks to appear in pictures that showed them looting a store. These posed photographs were printed in magazines and used as evidence of black criminality.

A few days after the fire, a light-skinned black newspaper reporter from New York asked Johnson to review an article she had written about the fire. They met in a secluded area of a park and sat on a bench

Not only was Jacksonville, Florida, devastated by the 1901 fire that consumed Johnson's school, but the disaster led to a heightening of racial tensions in the town. Johnson himself was attacked by a white mob a few days after the fire took place.

while Johnson read the article. As they were leaving the park, they were met by a screaming mob that included militiamen and bloodhounds. Johnson immediately understood the situation: He was in the park with a woman whom they thought was white. The mob seized and beat him, and he was dragged off to police headquarters.

When confronted with the truth, the civil authorities apologized to Johnson and his companion and released them. However, the incident would continue to trouble Johnson for many years. It impressed upon him how strongly racial problems were affected by public reaction against relations between black men and white women.

The rebuilding of the Stanton School began soon after the fire. Intent on getting away from the racial tensions in their hometown, Johnson and his brother left for New York again in June 1901. A few days after their arrival, they arranged a benefit concert that raised $1,000 for the Jacksonville relief fund. Rejoining Cole, they launched into a summer of composing. This time, the Cole and Johnson Brothers songwriting team soon became well known on Broadway.

The Johnsons began their songwriting careers at a time when the music of black performers was gaining increasing popularity. During the mid-19th century, black minstrel troupes traveled across the country popularizing ballads and humorous tunes about life on southern plantations. This was followed by the popularity of vaudeville shows, which offered comic routines that often featured songs by black composers. By the turn of the century, songs that presented stereotyped images of blacks had become very popular. However, composers such as Scott Joplin were beginning to win a place for a more spirited and serious type of music originated by blacks. This music had a syncopated, or ragged, beat, and was known as ragtime.

The songs of Cole and the Johnson Brothers featured the simple tunes of the then-popular songs, but they avoided unfavorable racial images. Although Johnson's lyrics used black dialect, they usually focused on such themes as love and courtship.

During the summer of 1901, Cole and the Johnson Brothers were asked to compose songs for a number of shows, including *The Sleeping Beauty and the Beast* and *The Supper Club*. Among the more popular of their compositions were "Nobody's Lookin' But the Owl and the Moon," "My Castle on the Nile," and "The Maiden with the Dreamy Eyes," which was an extremely successful love ballad. It was introduced by the singer Anna Held, who was the wife of the influential producer of the Broadway show *The Follies*, Florenz Ziegfeld.

With their star clearly on the rise, the trio signed a three-year contract with Joseph Stern and Company. However, sheet-music sales of their songs started slowly, and by January 1902, they were shocked to discover that they were in debt to Stern.

Early in 1902, the construction work on the Stanton School was completed. Johnson returned to Jacksonville, and Rosamond remained with Cole in New York. Johnson became extremely upset when he saw that the school was now housed in a shoddy new building. Although the school was located in one of the best sections of Jacksonville, the town council was seeking to move it to a less desirable area. Consequently, the council had apportioned money for a temporary structure.

Johnson fought with the town administrators to get them to construct a suitable building on the old site. He won the fight when it was discovered that the deed to the property required that the land be used for a school. Despite this victory, he was criticized by members of Jacksonville's black community for not paying enough attention to his duties as Stanton's principal. Admitting this charge to be true, he

When Bob Cole and Rosamond made tours of music halls around the country, they performed "Lazy Moon" and other numbers written by the songwriting team. The covers of the sheet music of the team's songs often bore the pictures of the singers who had helped to make the songs popular.

The song-and-dance team of Bert Williams (left) and George Walker helped to popularize black musical comedies on the vaudeville entertainment circuit. Walker and the Johnson brothers lived at the Marshall Hotel in New York City, which was a favorite meeting place for Broadway entertainers.

vowed to devote himself to his career in education. He had been elected president of the Florida State Teachers' Association during the previous year; he would begin to study for a lifetime teaching certification, which would relieve him of all requirements to take further examinations.

While Johnson was studying for his teaching examination during the summer of 1902, he still retained a desire to be part of the life on Broadway. When he received two checks from Rosamond with a note stating that the royalty payments for their songs were beginning to roll in, his resolve to remain in education disappeared. He hurriedly packed his bags and left for New York.

When Johnson arrived in New York, he was surprised at Rosamond and Cole's new appearance. They now owned dozens of fancy shirts, ties, and shoes. Next to them, Johnson admitted, "I felt like a country cousin."

Rosamond and Cole were busy staging a two-man vaudeville show in a New York theater. They appeared on stage in dress suits, pretending that they were rehearsing for a performance they would give at a party later that night. The two men started their act with classical music and then launched into several original pieces. Witnessing the success of Cole and the Johnson Brothers' songs convinced Johnson that he should devote himself to songwriting.

In September 1902, Johnson resigned from his position at the Stanton School. Although it was a difficult decision for him to reach, he realized that there was little chance that he could rise much further in the teaching profession. However, his prospects as a songwriter were almost unlimited.

After Cole and the Johnson Brothers' fame grew and they were able to afford comfortable quarters, they took up residence in the Marshall Hotel, a four-story building located on West 53rd Street. The hotel soon became a gathering place for black artists. Among those who often stayed there was the acclaimed comic singer and dancer Bert Williams.

Johnson worked hard on the lyrics to the team's songs and produced another big hit, "Under the Bamboo Tree," in 1902. He was often left alone to work on his compositions while Cole and Rosamond toured the country with their show. Yet he also found the time to attend parties held by New York's leading black families. At one of them, the lyricist of popular love songs met Grace Nail, the daughter of a successful pub owner and real estate investor. Impressed with her intelligence and knowledge of cultural affairs, he would see her often over the next few years.

Johnson also spent his time by taking courses in dramatic literature at Columbia University. His professor, Brander Matthews, was a leading literary critic as well as a great fan of Broadway shows and of Johnson's songs. Matthews persuaded Johnson to work at writing poems and stories that described the lives of black Americans. Johnson subsequently began to work on a novel about a black man who could pass as white.

The songwriting team of Cole and the Johnson Brothers worked hard to write songs that did not feature the coarse and demeaning lyrics that were then very popular. According to Rosamond, their songs retained "all that is distinctive in the old Negro music and yet which shall be sophisticated enough to appeal to the cultured musician." In 1903, they presented a series of songs called *The Evolution of Ragtime*, that traced the development of black music from spirituals and folk songs to minstrel shows to ragtime. By then, Cole and the Johnson Brothers had become one of the leading songwriting teams in New York. Nearly every successful Broadway show had one of their songs in it. "Under the Bamboo Tree" had sold more than 400,000 copies, and "Congo Love Song" was beginning to sell quite well.

While Johnson was living in New York, in the early 1900s, he was encouraged to begin work on a novel by Professor Brander Matthews (shown here), who taught literature at Columbia University.

Johnson was deeply impressed by the lack of racial prejudice displayed by the people whom he met while he was in England.

The team worked for a number of producers before signing a contract with Klaw and Erlanger, an acclaimed theatrical production company. One of their major assignments for this company was the writing of songs for the musical *Humpty Dumpty*, which was staged in November 1904.

Even though there was an increasing number of black musical shows, black theatergoers continued to be relegated to undesirable seats in many theaters. On several occasions when Johnson went to the theater, he had arguments with theater attendants who tried to move him from his seat. He also experienced the humiliation of being refused rides in hotel passenger elevators and of being barred from eating in some New York restaurants.

In the summer of 1905, Rosamond and Cole's act was engaged for a six-week show at London's Palace Theatre. Johnson chose to go along on the trip. The three of them decided to start their trip early and see Europe as tourists. Johnson was impressed by the lack of racial discrimination he encountered while in France and Belgium. He said that he felt "free from special scorn, special tolerance, special condescension . . . free to be merely a man." However, he noticed that the white Americans in Europe still bore racial prejudices.

The Palace Theatre in London provided an opulent contrast to the New York vaudeville show houses. The theater had a 40-piece orchestra and large placards announcing the appearance of the Cole and Johnson show; the theatergoers came to the performance wearing extremely fine clothing. Johnson was gratified by the audience's enthusiastic response to the show, and he was proud of the outstanding example that his brother and Cole made for black American performers.

The London tour was successful. However, at the end of the summer, Cole and the Johnson Brothers were in financial straits, having spent far more money than they had earned on the trip. To bring in some quick cash, they sold some songs to British theatrical producers. On the voyage home, Johnson became quite embarrassed when he discovered that he did not have enough money to leave respectable tips for the ship's personnel and had to borrow money from another passenger in order to do so.

After returning to New York, Johnson worked on the lyrics for a new musical, *The Shoo-Fly Regiment*, that Cole and Rosamond intended to present with a large touring company. They asked Johnson to join the tour as business manager. Worried that a large company would be too expensive to maintain, he also believed that the taxing job of business manager would absorb too much of his time and energy. He had written the lyrics to more than 200 successful songs during his 7 years as a songwriter, and he wanted a new challenge. In the spring of 1906, he ended his association with Cole and the Johnson Brothers. It was time to pursue a new career. ✺

4

DIPLOMATIC
VENTURES

◈

WHEN JOHNSON ANNOUNCED in 1902 that he was giving up his post as principal of the Stanton School and devoting himself to songwriting, many of his friends tried to persuade him to change his mind. They argued that a career on Broadway was not respectable enough for someone with his experience in school administration, legal work, and community service. After leaving his post, Johnson often wondered if he had made the right decision. Perhaps he had strayed from the course he had set for himself in college—to be a leader of his race.

Yet Johnson did not stray completely from a life of public service. While he was in New York, he became friends with the city's leading black politician, Charles Anderson, the president of the Colored Republican Club. Anderson owed much of his political power to his association with Booker T. Washington, America's most influential black spokesman. Washington served as an adviser on race relations to President Theodore Roosevelt and was skilled at gaining government jobs for his supporters. He was also adept at undermining his opponents in the black leadership, many of whom believed that his programs encouraged blacks to be too submissive toward discriminatory laws.

After Johnson joined the U.S. diplomatic corps in 1906, he served in several consulates in Latin America. Shown here is a turn-of-the-century view of the main street in downtown Caracas, the capital of Venezuela—the country where he was first stationed.

The most prominent black American leader in the early 1900s, Booker T. Washington (shown here) used his influence with the Republican administration in Washington, D.C., to help Johnson gain a position in the State Department.

Like many black Americans, Johnson supported the Republicans, the party of Abraham Lincoln, in the 1904 presidential elections. He helped Anderson's drive to win black support for the presidential bid of Roosevelt, the Republican candidate, writing with Rosamond two campaign songs, "You're All Right, Teddy" and "The Old Flag Never Touched the Ground." Anderson urged Johnson to become further involved in politics, and he soon accepted the position of treasurer of the Colored Republican Club. His Marshall Hotel residence was located opposite the club headquarters, and he often brought his friends over to the club to give concerts during membership drives.

After Roosevelt was voted back into office in 1904, Washington asked the president to appoint Anderson to an important government post. The few patronage positions given to blacks were usually of low rank. However, Roosevelt appreciated Anderson's past help and appointed him to a major government position in New York's financial district.

When Anderson assumed his new position in 1905, he asked Johnson to serve as president of the Colored Republican Club. Anderson also recommended to Washington that he use his influence to get Johnson a post overseas in a U.S. consulate, describing Johnson as "a man of sound judgment, ripe scholarship, with a character free from every stain." Anderson stated that it would help the black community to have the cultured, intelligent Johnson representing his race abroad and in the State Department. Johnson's fluency in the Spanish language made him a natural choice for a consular post in a Latin American country.

By the time Johnson was offered a diplomatic post in early 1906, he had decided to give up songwriting. He knew that the consular service was a low-paying profession and that he would be assigned to some out-of-the-way post that was reserved for blacks. However, he believed that if he was patient, he would be able to rise to a high position within the diplomatic corps.

At a banquet on May 10, 1906, 80 of Johnson's friends gathered to bid him good luck in his new career. Two days later, he said farewell to the cosmopolitan life of New York and left to take up his post as U.S. consul in Puerto Cabello, Venezuela.

The country was ruled by an iron-fisted, luxury-loving dictator, General Cipriano Castro, who had risen from his peasant background to become president. Castro, like the majority of Venezuelans, resented the strong economic control that the United States and the European nations exerted over their country. Nevertheless, Johnson got along well with the Venezuelans. Most of the population were of mixed

Johnson was attracted to the diplomatic service because it offered prestige and an opportunity to experience new cultures. He was impressed by the relative lack of racial prejudice among the Venezuelans, a group of whom are shown here on a street in Caracas.

In May 1906, Johnson began his diplomatic career as the superintendent of the U.S. consulate in the small port town of Puerto Cabello, Venezuela. He is shown here standing on the consulate's second-floor balcony.

Spanish, Indian, and African ancestry, and he was impressed by the relative lack of racial barriers in the country. He soon settled into the town's leisurely pace, and as consul, he prepared reports on local commerce and obtained clearance papers for American ships that visited the port.

Johnson carried out his duties conscientiously and often socialized with other foreign diplomats. He had much free time to write, and he was able to complete a number of poems, including "O Black and Unknown Bards" and "Mother Night," which were published in American magazines. He also wrote part of *The Autobiography of an Ex-Colored Man*, a novel about the life of a light-skinned black man that he had begun in New York.

Although Johnson valued his stay in Venezuela, he constantly pressed for a transfer to a higher post. When he was passed over for a choice assignment in Europe on one occasion, he was sure that a race riot involving a black army regiment in Brownsville, Texas, had caused race to be an issue in his bid for the post and thus had jeopardized his chance to be promoted. During such times of high racial tensions, positions in the government that were open to blacks became scarcer than usual.

When Johnson returned to New York at the end of 1906 on a two-month leave of absence, he found that the city had lost much of its appeal to him. Rosamond and Cole's national tour with *The Shoo-Fly Regiment* was a financial disaster, as he had feared it would be. His friends had left the Marshall Hotel and had moved elsewhere. However, his relationship with Grace Nail began to blossom.

When Johnson returned to Puerto Cabello, he discovered that a movement to unseat President Castro was developing. In 1908, Vice-president Vicente Gomez overthrew Castro while the president was in Europe undergoing a medical operation. Soon after

this happened, Johnson was given a promotion and assigned to a newly opened consulate in Corinto, Nicaragua. He traveled to Washington, D.C., in April 1909 so that he could be informed about his new post. He also stopped off at New York to see Grace Nail as well as Rosamond and Cole's new show, *The Red Moon*.

Johnson was unimpressed with Corinto, a busy port on the Pacific Ocean, when he first saw the Nicaraguan town in May 1909. However, he knew his position as consul was a very sensitive one. Nicaragua held strategic importance for the United States as a potential route for a canal between the Atlantic and Pacific oceans. The United States had already

After Johnson pressed the State Department to give him a more important post, he was reassigned to the American consulate in Corinto, Nicaragua, in May 1909. A group of American citizens are shown here holding umbrellas to protect themselves from the fierce tropical sun on a wharf at Corinto.

begun to build a canal in Panama, but other areas in other countries—including Nicaragua—were being considered as possible construction sites because the work was proceeding slowly.

As consul, Johnson knew that Nicaraguans had good reason to fear U.S. intervention in their country; Americans had long maintained strong financial interests there. In 1855, an American soldier of fortune named William Walker had taken control of the country and ruled it until he was deposed and executed in 1860. Since 1893, Nicaragua had been ruled by General José Santos Zelaya, a dictator who was often at odds with the U.S. government.

Johnson was therefore busy in his new post, and he kept a close eye on political developments in Nicaragua. Two months after he arrived, one of Zelaya's rivals, General Juan Estrada, started a revolution to overthrow the dictator. The American government openly supported Estrada and stationed a warship in Corinto's harbor. However, Zelaya managed to remain firmly in control in the capital at Managua.

In October 1909, Johnson took another leave of

Nicaragua was rocked by a series of political coups and experienced many changes of government during Johnson's stay there. American sailors, including the one shown here standing next to Johnson, were used to maintain order in Corinto.

absence and returned to the United States. After stopping in Washington, D.C., to inform his superiors in the State Department about developments in Nicaragua, he went to New York to complete a special personal mission: to propose marriage to Grace Nail. She accepted his proposal, and they were wed on February 3, 1910. A few weeks later, they sailed for Nicaragua.

Johnson was apprehensive about how his refined, cosmopolitan wife would react to the rough living conditions in Corinto. Yet she gradually became accustomed to the town, and she soon earned a reputation as a popular hostess. Even so, Johnson's desire for a post in Europe grew ever stronger.

While Johnson had been in the United States, the revolution against Zelaya had gained strength. The United States severed diplomatic relations with his government after he executed two Americans whom he accused of aiding the rebels. Zelaya's regime subsequently collapsed; he fled to Corinto, where he boarded a ship for refuge overseas. General Estrada replaced Zelaya as the country's new president.

After only four months in power, President Estrada lost control of his government. One night in May 1911, Johnson was awakened by a knocking on the door of the consulate. The frightened Estrada was outside, asking for asylum. A few days later, the ex-president fled abroad. In the wake of his flight, the former vice-president, Adolfo Diaz, became president. However, Diaz's power was soon threatened by two rivals.

In the midst of this uncertain situation, Johnson received a leave of absence. In November 1911, he and his wife returned to the United States. Stopping in Washington, D.C., Johnson entered another request in the State Department to be transferred to a post in Europe. He was told that he was being considered for a consular position in France. Continuing

Grace Nail first met Johnson at a dance in Brooklyn, New York. They were wedded several years later, in 1910.

on to New York, he arranged for the publication of the novel that he had recently completed. He then went to pay his final respects to Cole, who had drowned himself in the summer of 1911, depressed by the failure of his last show, *The Red Moon*.

Believing that he would soon be posted to France, Johnson returned to Nicaragua without Grace in March 1912. Soon after his return, a revolution broke out against President Diaz. Instead of fleeing from office, as Estrada had done, Diaz asked for U.S. military aid against the rebels. The American government sent warships and troops to Corinto.

Johnson skillfully performed his consular duties during the rebellion. In August 1912, with Corinto on the verge of falling to the rebels, he conducted negotiations with the rebel leaders that stalled an attack long enough for American reinforcements to arrive. His adept handling of the crisis gave him high hopes for an immediate transfer out of Central America.

By the fall of 1912, more than 2,000 marines were stationed in Nicaragua. With the help of U.S. troops, Diaz defeated the rebel forces, and Nicaragua became a U.S. protectorate. The country's economy and government remained in American control until 1926.

In November 1912, Johnson returned to the United States so that he could act as executor of the estate of his father, who had died while Johnson was in Nicaragua. He then discovered that his novel, *The Autobiography of an Ex-Colored Man*, had been published. He had chosen to have the novel published anonymously, believing that the work would have a greater impact if it was thought to be a true story.

The Autobiography of an Ex-Colored Man features an unnamed narrator who tells the story of his life. The light-skinned son of a mulatto mother and white father, he passes first as a white musician and then as a black musician, learning all the while about his

Although The Autobiography of an Ex-Colored Man *did not receive much attention when it was published in 1912, Johnson's novel strongly influenced the writers who took part in the Harlem Renaissance during the 1920s.*

1/10/12

Banquet and Reception

IN HONOR OF

HON. JAS. W. JOHNSON

U. S. Consul--Corinto Nicaragua

and

J. ROSAMOND JOHNSON, Esq.

of New York City, N. Y.

GIVEN BY

The Citizens of Jacksonville, Florida

in Bethel Baptist Institutional Church

Wednesday, Jan. 10th, 1912

During a leave of absence from his consular duties in 1912, Johnson and his brother, Rosamond, attended a banquet given in their honor by the leading citizens of Jacksonville's black community.

different racial heritages. Horrified by the indignities that blacks must endure, he chooses to live as a white man. However, he ultimately regrets that in rejecting his dual identity, he has lost part of his soul.

The novel was partly based on the life of Judson Wetmore, Johnson's former law partner in Jacksonville. In the novel, Johnson sought to dispel racial stereotypes while depicting the harmful prejudices that governed relations between blacks and whites. He also tried to evoke the magnetic energy possessed by evangelical preachers and black spirituals.

The Autobiography of an Ex-Colored Man received little attention when it was first published. The book did not reach a large audience until the late 1920s, after the black cultural movement known as the Harlem Renaissance had begun to create a great interest in works on racial struggles. By then, the novel featured an introduction by Carl Van Vechten, a white critic and writer who was instrumental in helping many black artists win public recognition.

During Johnson's last months in Nicaragua, he had also worked feverishly to complete a poem about the Emancipation Proclamation in time for the celebration of its 50th anniversary on January 1, 1913. The poem, "Fifty Years," was published on the editorial page of the *New York Times*, and it won immediate acclaim for its stirring verses on the themes of black pride and racial harmony. In the poem, Johnson championed the rights of blacks to receive the full benefits of American citizenship, especially in lines such as:

> This land is ours by right of birth,
> This land is ours by right of toil;
> We helped to turn its virgin earth,
> Our sweat is in its fruitful soil.

Johnson spent the following months in Jacksonville trying to settle his father's estate, which was tied up by legal problems involving investments in a bankrupt company. He asked for an extension on his leave of absence from the State Department but by the middle of 1913, he was beginning to question whether he wanted to remain in the consular service. The Democratic candidate, Woodrow Wilson, had won the 1912 presidential election, and all appointments to government offices were therefore in the hands of a Democratic administration. The new secretary of state, William Jennings Bryan, told Johnson that he would have to remain in his old post at Corinto.

Johnson was disappointed that he was again being assigned to Nicaragua. He realized that with the Democrats in power in Washington, D.C., a black Republican such as himself had little chance for promotions within the consular service. "I was up against politics plus race prejudice," he maintained. Consequently, he resigned from the consular service in September 1913. At the age of 42, he was going to have to start a new career once more. ❧

When President Woodrow Wilson (shown here) assumed power in 1913, Johnson knew that a black Republican such as himself would have little chance for advancement within the diplomatic corps. He resigned from the State Department later that year.

The CRISIS

THE
AMERICAN NEGRO'S RECORD IN THE GREAT
WORLD WAR

LOYALTY

VALOR

ACHIEVEMENT

ONE DOLLAR A YEAR   MAY 1919   TEN CENTS A COPY

5

BODY AND SOUL

J OHNSON DID NOT have any definite ideas about what kind of work he wanted to do after he left the consular service late in the summer of 1913. Because *The Autobiography of an Ex-Colored Man* was selling poorly, he felt that he probably would not be able to make a living as a writer. He and Grace remained in Jacksonville for more than a year with his mother, who was in very poor health. He was offered his former job as the Stanton School's principal, but he turned it down. For a while, he wrote scripts for a local filmmaking company, but he was soon repelled by the films' treatment of blacks and decided to look for other work.

Helen Johnson hoped that her son would remain in Jacksonville. However, Johnson was disturbed by the increasingly hostile racial climate there and by the hardening of the Jim Crow system throughout the South. In the fall of 1914, he and his wife moved back to New York and took up residence in Harlem, where Grace's family was living. Johnson again tried songwriting with Rosamond, but he realized that he had lost the touch for writing popular lyrics.

An interesting job opportunity soon opened up for Johnson. The *New York Age*, a leading black weekly newspaper with a large national readership, was looking for someone to write a column for its editorial

The cover to an issue of The Crisis, *a periodical published by the National Association for the Advancement of Colored People (NAACP), celebrates the heroism of black soldiers during World War I. Johnson proved to be a highly successful recruiter for the organization.*

page. The paper's editor, Fred Moore, believed that Johnson's wide background made him an ideal candidate for the job and offered the position to him. Johnson eagerly accepted it.

In October 1914, Johnson wrote the first of a series of editorials that would last for 10 years. In his columns, he attacked a wide range of abuses that were being perpetrated against blacks throughout the country. He advocated a policy of nonviolence coupled with political and economic pressure to force changes in discriminatory laws. His columns alerted readers to new legislation that advanced Jim Crow policies, and they were effective in fostering a growing spirit of defiance in the black community.

Johnson's editorials sought to spur action that would reverse the status of black Americans. In the South, blacks lived under extreme oppression. More than 3,000 southern blacks were lynched between 1890 and 1920, and the criminals almost always went unpunished. Jim Crow laws enforced strict racial segregation; restrictive voting rights laws kept blacks from exercising any political power. Johnson saw little difference between the position of impoverished sharecroppers in the 1910s and slaves in the pre– Civil War South.

Blacks who moved from farms in the South and sought jobs in the North's industrialized cities found only slightly better conditions. White workers felt threatened by the influx of black labor and stirred up racial hostility. Blacks were forced to take the lowest-paying jobs and were crowded into the poorest and most unsanitary sections of the northern cities.

To reverse the increasingly worsening racial situation in the United States, Johnson urged blacks to make a bid for racial justice that would be founded upon a "concerted effort inspired by high courage and idealism." But he knew that for such an effort to succeed, some degree of cooperation between the leaders of the various black rights organizations was imperative.

At that time, the black leadership was divided into different factions. The strongest of these was the Tuskegee group, which included influential figures such as Charles Anderson and educator Robert Moton. The group was led by Booker T. Washington, founder and director of a black vocational school in Tuskegee, Alabama, who urged blacks to better their condition by obtaining job skills that would open further employment opportunities for them within the American economy. Washington did not believe in organized protest movements, fearing that such actions would stir up racial animosity. He believed instead that blacks should accommodate themselves to segregation. He therefore enjoyed the confidence of many white leaders.

After Johnson left the consular service in 1913, he spent some time with his mother in Jacksonville, Florida, before settling in Harlem, where he and his wife lived near her family. He is shown here with Grace (center), her mother, and her brother, Jack (at rear).

Educator and author W. E. B. Du Bois (shown here) was the editor of the NAACP's The Crisis. Johnson said of him, "Du Bois in battle is a stern, bitter, relentless fighter, who, when he has put aside his sword, is among his particular friends the most jovial and fun-loving of men."

Washington and his associates in the Tuskegee group had dominated black politics for some time. However, by 1914, their position was being challenged by younger leaders, many of whom supported the newly formed National Association for the Advancement of Colored People (NAACP). This organization took an unyielding stand against all discriminatory laws and called for stronger laws to combat lynching. W. E. B. Du Bois, the organization's director of publicity and research and editor of its official organ, *The Crisis,* was a strong critic of Washington's accommodationist policies. He called for the formation of a "talented tenth" of black leaders who would direct a national campaign for black rights.

Most of the NAACP's membership was black, but all of the executive staff except for Du Bois were white. Many of the executive members were among the civil rights activists who had signed "The Call," a letter printed in the *New York Evening Post* on February 12, 1909—the 100th anniversary of Abraham Lincoln's birthday. The signers of the letter had been horrified by the reports of a race riot in Lincoln's hometown of Springfield, Illinois, and had called for a national campaign to rid the country of racial violence and inequality.

Shortly after the publication of the letter, a group of prominent black and white leaders met in New York and formed the National Negro Congress, which in 1911 changed its name to the NAACP. Working with only a small budget, the NAACP struggled during its early years to build a national organization that could help blacks achieve voting rights and educational opportunities. Through *The Crisis,* newsletters, and lectures, the NAACP sought to spread its message of racial equality throughout the United States. When Washington died in 1915, the NAACP found that the time was ripe to expand its influence.

Johnson became interested in the NAACP's programs while writing editorials for the *New York Age*. In 1916, he began to go to NAACP meetings in New York, and he was soon elected vice-president of the local branch. In August of that same year, Du Bois and two other leaders of the NAACP held a conference in Amenia, New York, in the hope of uniting the different strands of the black rights movement. Johnson was one of the 50 people who attended the Amenia Conference and pledged to commit themselves to winning full political and educational rights for blacks.

With the hope of uniting the black leadership behind its programs, the NAACP started searching

Johnson (back row, fifth from left) was among many of the leading members of the civil rights movement who met at a conference in Amenia, New York, in 1916 to discuss ways of promoting racial equality.

On July 28, 1917, a few weeks after a mob attack on the black community in East Saint Louis, Illinois, Johnson and the NAACP staged a parade of black organizations down Fifth Avenue in New York City to protest the mob violence.

for a dynamic recruiter who could greatly increase the organization's membership. The NAACP board decided that the respected, well-spoken Johnson was the best candidate and offered the job to him. He was thrilled by the offer, stating that "every bit of experience I had had, from the principalship of Stanton School to the editorship on The New York Age, was preparation for the work I was being asked to undertake."

In December 1916, Johnson became the NAACP's field secretary. His associates on the executive board included prominent white liberals such as Joel and Arthur Spingarn, Mary White Ovington, Moorfield Storey, and Oswald Garrison Villard. Roy Nash, the executive secretary, was in charge of day-to-day affairs. These white executives—lawyers, professors, writers, and social workers who were strongly committed to establishing racial equality in the United States—provided a link to important financial and political power sources. They served the organization as unpaid volunteers but did not compose a full-time professional staff.

As field secretary, Johnson's duties included setting up branches of the organization and recruiting new members. The NAACP had fewer than 9,000 members in 1916; only 3 of its 70 branches were located in the South, where the bulk of the country's black population lived. Two months after becoming field secretary, Johnson embarked on an exhausting membership drive, visiting 15 cities in the South to organize new branches and seeking out civil rights supporters of both races. He was intent on "hammering at white America," but he knew that for racial equality to be achieved "it would be necessary to awaken black America."

Johnson contacted black churches, schools, and fraternal and professional organizations to recruit new members. He worked especially hard to recruit well-educated, middle-class blacks into the NAACP, hoping that they would provide strong community leadership. His early efforts were successful, and more branches were opened in the South. He made numerous additional trips throughout the country, and his name drew many prospective members to NAACP branch meetings. Three years after he became field secretary, the NAACP grew to 310 branches and 100,000 members.

Johnson drew many talented young men and old associates into the NAACP. George Towns, a friend from Atlanta University, became the leader of the Georgia NAACP organization and made impressive gains in recruiting members from the isolated black communities in small rural towns. He also led drives to get blacks to register to vote and to increase financial support for black schools.

Johnson discovered that in some areas of the United States—especially in the South—blacks looked to the NAACP as a means of salvation from their oppressors. On many occasions, Johnson felt anguished about his inability to shield blacks from the atrocities that were committed against them with depressing frequency. But he still tried hard to convince people that only a well-coordinated national organization such as the NAACP could push for legislation that would give blacks some protection.

In 1917, Johnson made a trip to Memphis, Tennessee, to investigate a white mob's burning of a black man who was accused without any sure evidence of being an ax murderer. After visiting the site of the lynching, Johnson described his feelings:

> A pile of ashes and pieces of charred wood still marked the spot. While the ashes were yet hot, the bones had been scrambled for as souvenirs by the mobs. . . . I tried to balance the sufferings of the miserable victim against the moral degradation of Memphis, and the

Although most black Americans supported their country's war effort during World War I, only limited progress was made in the civil rights causes for which Johnson was fighting. Jim Crow laws in the South went so far as to state where blacks could wait for taxis.

truth flashed over me that in large measure, the race question involves the saving of black America's body and white America's soul.

Johnson's travels as the NAACP's field secretary were both mentally and physically draining. Consequently, he found little time for creative writing, although he did continue his weekly column for the *New York Age* and in 1917 published *Fifty Years and Other Poems*, a collection of poems that he had written during the previous 30 years. The book did not become very popular. However, some of the poems on racial themes, such as "O Southland," "Brothers," and "To America," received strong praise.

When the United States entered World War I in April 1917, several of the NAACP's leaders—including Roy Nash—enlisted in the army. Johnson was asked by the NAACP board members to serve as acting executive secretary until someone could be found to replace Nash. Although Johnson was more interested in his organizing work as field secretary, he agreed to take the position.

During World War I, more than 380,000 black soldiers enlisted in America's armed forces and fought with distinction. At first, no training program for black officers existed. Joel Spingarn of the NAACP eventually helped to establish a separate camp for blacks in Des Moines, Iowa. At this camp, 678 blacks became commissioned officers. Spingarn was criticized by some members of the NAACP for accepting an arrangement that resulted in a segregated camp. However, the army adamantly refused to approve integrated training programs.

When the war created a labor shortage in the country's large industrial centers, many blacks moved to northern cities in search of jobs. In some places, the white population engaged in all-out attacks on the growing black communities. On July 2, 1917, in East St. Louis, Illinois, more than 100 blacks were killed and thousands more were forced from their homes as a result of a horrifyingly destructive race riot. Similar incidents occurred in other parts of the country. In many cases, blacks were indicted for causing the riots. Johnson and other NAACP members were kept busy arranging legal assistance for the defendants and funding for the homeless.

On July 28, 1917, Johnson and others at the NAACP organized a silent march to protest these acts of violence. More than 10,000 blacks marched on Fifth Avenue in New York carrying banners that read, "Mother, do lynchers go to heaven?" and "Treat us so that we may love our country." The parade helped to unite the black protest movement.

Less than a month later, another crisis erupted when black soldiers in Houston, Texas, rioted after one of their officers was beaten by the local police. Two blacks and 17 whites were killed during the fighting. Thirteen soldiers were convicted of murder and were quickly executed; others were also sentenced to death or to long prison sentences. Johnson led a delegation to Washington, D.C., to ask President Wilson to grant pardons to the remaining soldiers. Wilson listened to the delegation's pleas and then ordered that the cases be reviewed by the War Department. Although six more men were executed, some of the soldiers were given lighter sentences.

Johnson did not condone rioting, but he was angered that the American government refused to help blacks gain full justice. After the Houston affair, he gave a stirring speech at Carnegie Hall in New York in which he called on America to stand up for its black citizens, so many of whom were defending the nation's flag on the battlegrounds of Europe. Before a loudly cheering audience, he cried out that acts of racial injustice stained the flag, and he concluded, "They dim its stars and soil its stripes; wash them out! wash them out!"

In the fall of 1917, Johnson's mother became seriously ill in Jacksonville. He moved her to New York, where she remained until her death on January 7, 1918. After she was buried in New York, Johnson and Rosamond had their father's body brought north so that their parents could lie together in the city where they first met.

In the spring of 1918, a white social worker named John Shillady was appointed executive secretary of the NAACP, and Johnson returned to his recruiting work. He and Shillady worked well together, and a concerted membership drive added many new members. Johnson also began an effort to include more blacks on the NAACP executive board. Walter White, a young black leader from Atlanta, was one of those who worked at the organization's New York headquarters. He became Johnson's chief assistant and was put in charge of investigating lynching cases.

When World War I ended in November 1918,

W. E. B. Du Bois (standing at right) and the staff of The Crisis *were especially busy during the Red Summer of 1919, when the newspaper was filled with accounts of the racial violence that was sweeping the country following the end of World War I.*

As the national organizer for the NAACP, Johnson met with many of the country's most distinguished black leaders. He is shown here standing next to Robert Moton, who succeeded Booker T. Washington as the head of the Tuskegee Institute.

America's armaments industries cut production. The period that followed was marked by even greater racial tensions than the previous years as returning white soldiers demanded jobs and returning black soldiers demanded that they be treated with respect.

Bloody race riots broke out in Chicago, Washington, D.C., and other cities during the so-called Red Summer of 1919. Black communities defended themselves against the attacks of white mobs, but they still suffered huge losses. While Shillady, the executive secretary, voiced his protests through letters, Johnson assumed the active role of lobbyist in the nation's capital and urged an official investigation into the acts of racial violence. He accused the Washington, D.C., newspapers of starting the local riot through their sensationalized articles about acts of black lawlessness. Some of the newspapers eventually agreed to print editorials calling for an end to the racial tensions.

The increasing frequency of acts of racial violence led to an NAACP campaign to make lynching a federal offense. In 1919, the NAACP published *Thirty Years of Lynching (1889–1919)*, a book based on newspaper reports of lynchings during the period. The opponents of antilynching legislation often claimed that most of the blacks who had been killed were guilty of raping white women. However, the report's findings indicated many victims were lynched for "talking back" to a white and not moving from the road to let a white pass. Only a few cases involved charges of rape, which were never proved. In addition, many of the lynching victims were black women.

The NAACP members were met in many areas with hostility and violence. In August 1919, Shillady went to Austin, Texas, hoping to block an attempt by the state's attorney general to examine the local NAACP chapter's membership book. Shillady defended the NAACP's program before a group of Austin politicians, but after the discussion he was seized and badly beaten by a racist mob led by a county judge. The governor of Texas endorsed the violence, writing in a letter to Spingarn, "Your organization can contribute more to the advancement of both races by keeping your representatives and their propaganda out of this state." The Austin courts refused to prosecute Shillady's attackers.

The executive secretary was emotionally scarred by the experience. In April 1920, he resigned from his office, stating that he was no longer confident that the NAACP could quickly bring about racial equality in the United States. Johnson sympathized with the traumatized Shillady, but his observation of the atrocities that were committed daily against blacks had long ago convinced him that the battle against racial oppression would be long and difficult and should not be abandoned.

During Johnson's first four years with the NAACP, he had proved his value as an organizer, administrator, and spokesman. When the position of executive secretary became vacant after Shillady's resignation, Du Bois argued strongly that the next director of the NAACP should be black. He nominated Johnson, and most of the other board members agreed with his choice. In November 1920, Johnson was officially installed as the new executive secretary. He was ready for the long battle that lay ahead.

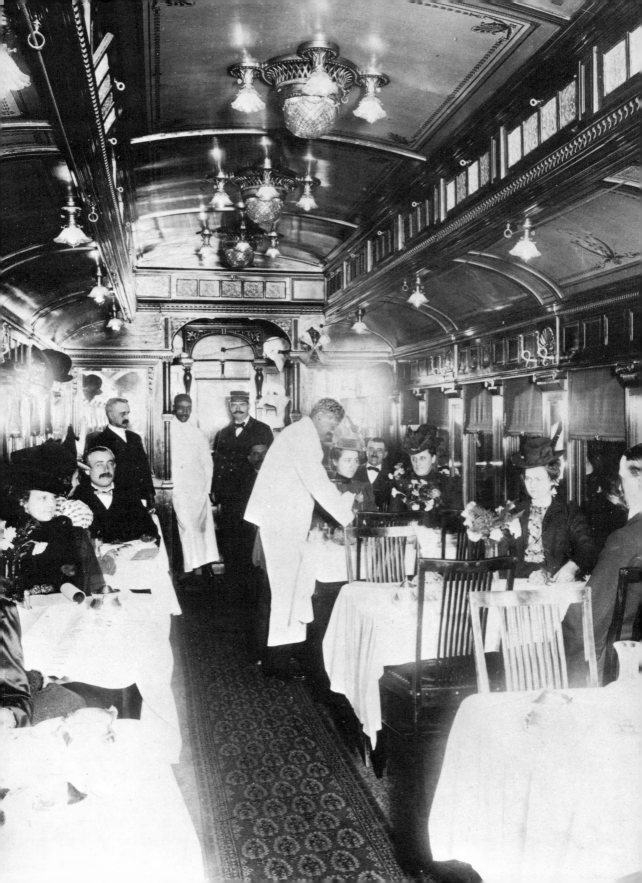

6

A TOWER
OF HOPES

T HE NAACP WAS experiencing a gradual
change in its policymaking structure when Johnson
was appointed the first permanent black executive
secretary in 1920. Although the white members on
the board of directors continued to play key advisory
roles in the NAACP's civil rights campaigns, more
and more of the work was being done by black members, such as Johnson, who had assumed salaried administrative positions. Johnson was committed to
maintaining the NAACP as an interracial body, but
he realized that much of the organizational and cor-
respondence work could only be performed by black
staff members.

Johnson provided the NAACP with strong leadership and a spirit of optimism about racial affairs
during his term in office. With his varied background
as a newspaper editor, author, teacher, songwriter,
and diplomat, he was able to appeal to people of many
different classes. His experience in the consular service and as president of the New York Colored Republican Club helped prepare him for lobbying work
in Washington, D.C. His former connections with
Booker T. Washington's group helped to reassure

*As part of the NAACP's campaign for civil rights during John-
son's term as executive secretary, the organization endorsed the efforts of black railroad employees—such as the ones shown here—
to win improvements in their working conditions.*

75

Johnson's chief assistant, Walter White (at far left), and field secretary William Pickens (third from right) were among the key members of the NAACP's administrative staff when Johnson served as the executive secretary.

conservative black leaders who would otherwise have been reluctant to join an organization that was agitating for civil rights bills.

Although Johnson was by nature reserved and somewhat cautious, he skillfully handled the Herculean task of coordinating the efforts of an underfinanced organization and its overworked staff. As requests for help poured in from NAACP branches around the country, Johnson and his co-workers reviewed each case, trying to determine which ones merited special consideration. The staff members at the NAACP headquarters in New York arranged for lawyers to represent local branches battling discriminatory voting laws or defending a black person whose legal rights were being violated. Johnson also created a strong publicity network to highlight racial abuses throughout the country. NAACP newsletters were sent to Congress, the press, and public organizations to keep up the pressure for national action on civil rights.

The energetic, dedicated people whom Johnson hired to fill positions on the NAACP staff were of immense help to him. He was especially dependent on his chief assistant, Walter White, who traveled to different crisis spots around the country in the 1920s and took charge of the local NAACP operations. White was also heavily involved with lobbying efforts at the nation's capital. Two other staff members—the field secretary, William Pickens, and the branch director, Robert Bagnall—worked hard to increase recruitment and invigorate the NAACP branches. Johnson also greatly appreciated the job done by Herbert Seligmann, the publicity director, who was adept at promoting the organization's civil rights campaigns. Lastly, Du Bois's militant articles in *The Crisis* helped to rally national support for racial equality.

Johnson's skillful use of newsletters, press releases, and articles in The Crisis *helped to stimulate national interest in the black struggle for equality.*

Crowds line a Harlem street as cars parading members of Marcus Garvey's Universal Negro Improvement Association pass by. Many blacks were drawn to Garvey's black nationalist organization in the years following World War I.

One of the first issues that Johnson became involved in during his term as executive secretary concerned the recent U.S. occupation of the black West Indian nation of Haiti, which had been self-governed since achieving its independence from France in 1803. After a civil war endangered American business and military interests there in 1915, the U.S. government sent troops to restore order. Johnson supported the invasion, believing that the United States had the right to prevent civil unrest from harming its interests in the Caribbean. However, when the United States established an occupation government in Haiti, he began to grow worried that the civil rights of the island's black population were being violated. In March 1920, he traveled to Haiti as part of an NAACP investigation of the U.S. occupation.

During his six weeks in Haiti, Johnson discovered numerous cases of atrocities committed by U.S. Marine troops against the native population. He was alarmed that the policies of the occupation force seemed to be largely directed by powerful American corporations that had little interest in the welfare of the black workers on the island's plantations. When he returned to the United States, Johnson wrote an influential report attacking the U.S. occupation of Haiti. After he became the head of the NAACP, he continued to press for the withdrawal of U.S. troops from Haiti. However, the American presence did not end until 1934.

A few months before Johnson became executive secretary, he led an NAACP delegation before Warren Harding, the Republican candidate in the 1920 presidential elections, to press for his support for civil rights legislation. Johnson told Harding that the NAACP was a well-organized machine that could gain many votes for the Republicans if the party committed itself to black causes. Harding, who in No-

In 1920, Johnson traveled to Haiti to investigate reports of atrocities committed by U.S. troops against civilians after the American occupation of the island in 1915. A crowded plaza in the Haitian capital of Port-Au-Prince is shown here.

vember would be swept into office with a Republican majority in both the Senate and the House of Representatives, was unwilling to provide strong public encouragement for racial equality measures because he feared that his party would lose its support in the South.

Nevertheless, Johnson remained hopeful that the Republican party would lead a national civil rights effort. Knowing that Congress would need constant prodding from black organizations, he sought to build a solid coalition out of the diverse groups that represented the black community. These efforts were only partially successful. Although the NAACP won the respect and support of a great number of blacks, many were also drawn to the black nationalist movement of Marcus Garvey and his Universal Negro Improvement Association. An outspoken critic of the NAACP's attempts to promote racial integration in American society, Garvey called on blacks to stop participating in white institutions and to look to Africa for their spiritual roots.

Much of Johnson's time was spent working on the NAACP's efforts to win passage of a congressional antilynching bill. From the initial work of the antilynching crusader Ida Wells-Barnett in the 1890s, the national campaign against the kidnapping and murdering of southern blacks had grown increasingly stronger. Two unsuccessful proposals for antilynching legislation were developed before L. C. Dyer, a congressman from Missouri, introduced a bill in April 1918 that would make lynching a federal offense. The bill allowed the federal government to provide protection for citizens if states refused to safeguard them from racial attacks, and it proposed measures for prosecuting individuals who engaged in mob violence.

The Dyer antilynching bill was finally reviewed by congressional committees in 1920, and the NAACP launched an intensive lobbying campaign to pressure congressmen to support the bill. Although Walter White directed the NAACP's operations in Washington, D.C., Johnson made frequent trips to the capital so that he could make direct use of his influence with politicians and the press. After two years of shuttling back and forth between New York and Washington, D.C., he stated that he had "tramped the corridors of the Capitol and the two office buildings so constantly that toward the end, I could, I think, have been able to find my way about blindfolded."

The bill was voted on first by the House of Representatives. The congressional debates gave vent to extreme outpourings of racial prejudice. Thomas Sisson, a congressman from Mississippi, attempted to use the false issue of rape as a means to inflame sympathies against the bill. He declared:

> No good man in the South believes in lynching as a method of enforcing law. But as long as rape continues, lynching will continue. . . . We are going to protect our girls and womenfolk from these black brutes.

Johnson and the NAACP provided the members of the House with reams of information about the true circumstances involving lynching cases. In January 1922, Johnson's organization celebrated as the Dyer bill passed in the House by a margin of 230 to 119.

To become law, the Dyer bill still had to be approved by the Senate, which was more conservative than the House. Many senators believed that the bill was unconstitutional because it infringed on rights guaranteed to state governments. Southern Democrats were eventually able to block the bill from even being voted on, and the antilynching legislation was defeated.

Looking back on his long, fruitless effort to push the Dyer bill through Congress, Johnson wrote, "Often

"If I could have my wish," Johnson said, "the Negro would retain his racial identity, with unhampered freedom to develop his own qualities—the best of those qualities American civilization is much in need of."

The 1920s witnessed a revival of the white supremacist organization known as the Ku Klux Klan, shown here staging a massive parade in Washington, D.C.

my tower of hopes came crashing down and had to be built up all over again. Sometimes my heart was as sore and weary as my feet." However, his work did bring results in many other cases. The NAACP brought suits that forced school boards to provide greater funding for black schools. Other victories were won when the courts in Louisville, Kentucky, ruled that racial discrimination in matters of housing was illegal and when the previously all-white Democratic primary in Texas was opened to black voters. Johnson also helped to bring about the removal of a clause in a congressional bill that would have outlawed interracial marriages.

During 1923, Johnson and the NAACP became heavily involved in a controversy over the staffing of a Veterans Bureau hospital in Tuskegee, Alabama. Built by the federal government as a facility for treating long-term injuries to black veterans of World War I, the Tuskegee hospital was originally supposed to be administrated by a mainly black medical staff. After local white organizations and the Ku Klux Klan, a white supremacist group, marched on the hospital's grounds and demanded that black personnel be excluded from the medical staff, the Veterans Bureau reversed its previous decision and appointed a white staff. The NAACP raised a howl of protest, claiming that the new Tuskegee staff was even providing sheets from the hospital's supplies for Klansmen to parade in. Pressure by the NAACP eventually led to the appointment of a black staff.

Another important case that the NAACP became involved in during Johnson's administration was the trial of a black family for murder in Detroit, Michigan. In 1925, a white mob attacked the residence of Ossian Sweet, a black physician who had just moved into a white neighborhood. During the attack, a shot was fired from the house, killing one person in the mob. Everyone in the house was arrested and charged with murder.

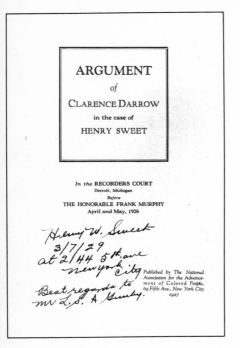

The NAACP provided legal assistance for noted lawyer Clarence Darrow's defense of Ossian Sweet and his family, who received national attention when they were put on trial for the death of a white man who was part of a mob that attacked their home.

The NAACP arranged for the prominent lawyer Clarence Darrow to represent the defendants in the Sweet case. Johnson began an extensive campaign for contributions that raised more than $75,000 for the NAACP legal defense fund. In 1927, the trial ended with the acquittal of all of the defendants.

During the 1920s, most labor unions refused to have black members because white workers were afraid to subject themselves to black competition. When white workers went on strike, their employers often heightened racial tensions by hiring black workers to replace them. In 1925, Johnson and the NAACP endorsed the efforts of labor organizer A. Philip Randolph to create a union of railroad car attendants, the mainly black Brotherhood of Sleeping Car Porters and Maids. Although Randolph's efforts were successful, Johnson's desire to avoid having the NAACP labeled as a radical organization limited the NAACP's participation in labor struggles.

Johnson's own labors proved to be extremely taxing. The NAACP constantly faced a financial struggle, and Johnson's influence with many philanthropic organizations helped to keep the association afloat. Within the NAACP, he maintained his position as a very popular leader. His success was based to a great extent on his skill at settling disputes within the NAACP and in encouraging all of the staff members to perform up to their potential. In 1925, his outstanding service to the NAACP and the black community was recognized when he was awarded the prestigious Spingarn Medal, the highest honor given to black Americans.

Although Johnson was proud of the dedicated, professional organization he had helped to build, by 1926, he was increasingly looking to other activities to find relief from the pressures of his administrative work. To obtain a refuge from the hectic pace of New York, he and Grace bought a rural estate in Great

Barrington, Massachusetts, that they named Five Acres. In addition, he worked on various writing projects during breaks from his NAACP affairs.

More and more, Johnson found the burdens of administrative work and his desire to pursue literary projects pressing on him. He was asked by the political leaders in Harlem to run as the Republican candidate for the House of Representatives, but he turned down the offer. In the spring of 1929, he fell ill from exhaustion and had to take leave of his work. After he returned, he was offered a fellowship from the Rosenwald Fund, a foundation that supports scholarly work. He decided to accept the offer of a grant to spend a year writing a book about black culture. Walter White took over as acting executive secretary of the NAACP.

Despite Johnson's heavy workload with the NAACP, he still found the time to work on literary projects and to relax.

In 1929, Johnson accepted a grant from the Rosenwald Foundation so that he could take a leave of absence from the NAACP and concentrate on his writing. Philanthropist Julius Rosenwald, the creator of the fellowship, is shown here with his wife.

Johnson greatly enjoyed the opportunity granted to him by the Rosenwald fellowship. In the fall of 1929, he traveled to Japan to take part in a conference on international affairs; the trip seemed to restore him to full health. After his return to America, he spent many productive months on his writing projects.

Johnson's leave of absence from the NAACP was scheduled to end in the fall of 1930, but by that summer he had begun to question whether he wanted to resume the secretaryship. Almost 60 years old, he decided that a less tiring job would be better for him. In December 1930, he announced that he was resigning as executive secretary of the NAACP to become a professor of creative literature at Fisk University in Nashville, Tennessee. The teaching position would leave him much time to write.

At a dinner organized by the NAACP board and staff in May 1931, more than 300 people—including Paul Robeson and painter Aaron Douglas—paid tribute to the man who had molded the organization into an effective tool against racial oppression. Johnson had successfully managed to get a number of disparate personalities to work toward a unified goal. Although only a few of his hopes for great strides in civil rights progress had been realized, a strong national network had been established to assure blacks that racial discrimination would not go unchallenged. The foundation had been laid for the great advances that would come in future years. ❧

"If the Negro is to fail, America fails with him," Johnson maintained. "If America wishes to make democratic institutions secure, she must deal with this question right and righteously."

7

THE SPIRIT OF
HARLEM

_____ •(•)• _____

URING JOHNSON'S YEARS as executive secretary of the NAACP, he also made impressive contributions to the development of black culture in the United States. His home in Harlem placed him at the center of the tremendous flowering of the arts that brought black literature, music, and painting into national prominence during the 1920s. This awakening of black artistic expression became known as the Harlem Renaissance.

There were many forces at work behind the emergence of Harlem as the center of black American culture in the 1920s. Beginning at the turn of the century, crop failures and racial oppression in the South spurred many black farmers to move north and look for jobs in New York City and other large northern industrial centers, where job opportunities were more plentiful than in the South. Real estate developers such as Grace's brother, John E. Nail, bought large sections of Harlem and encouraged blacks to move into the district's impressive brownstone buildings. Black churches left New York's midtown areas and built new structures in Harlem, bringing with them their congregations and age-old religious traditions. Businesses, fraternal organizations, social clubs,

During the 1920s, Harlem became a leading center of black culture and political activism. This flowering of black intellectualism prompted Johnson to produce anthologies and studies of the Harlem Renaissance.

political groups, and theaters joined the exodus to Harlem, and local newspapers such as the *New York Age* and *Amsterdam News* kept their readers informed about activities and trends in Harlem's fast-changing society.

The black population in Harlem included people from a wide variety of cultural backgrounds: native New Yorkers, midwesterners, southerners, and West Indians—many of whom prospered in their new setting in America's largest city. One of the results of this prosperity was the development of a cultured and educated black middle class that was interested in promoting the arts. A feeling of racial pride began to grow among Harlem's expanding black community, and the new spirit was captured by the district's bold young artists.

Harlem was not the only center of black culture in America. The black communities in Washington, D.C.; Cleveland, Ohio; New Orleans, Louisiana; and many other cities made major contributions to the

Harlem was a place of hope and opportunity to thousands of black Americans who moved there during the early 1900s. Many of them settled into huge tenement buildings such as this one, which was owned by Grace Johnson's brother, Jack.

arts. But Harlem was the premier center. Its glittering nightclubs lured people of all races to come and enjoy the wild dancing and exuberant music of the Jazz Age and the Roaring Twenties. People flocked to Harlem's entertainment clubs to see such stars as singers Bessie Smith, Ethel Waters, Roland Hayes, and Florence Mills; dancer Bill "Bojangles" Robinson; actors Charles Gilpin and Paul Robeson; and musicians Duke Ellington, Louis Armstrong, Fats Waller, and Fletcher Henderson. Black culture was suddenly in vogue in New York and many other areas of the country.

While audiences listened to jazz and danced to swing music, many people also began to take notice of the exciting literature being produced by Langston Hughes, Countee Cullen, Claude McKay, Zora Neale Hurston, Arna Bontemps, and the others in the generation of young black writers who sparked the Harlem Renaissance. Journals such as *The Crisis* and *Opportunity* gave many aspiring young black writers their first chance to find an audience. Many of them were influenced by the militant protest philosophy of W. E. B. Du Bois and by the growing movement toward greater racial consciousness. They were representatives of what scholar Alain Locke, an authority on the Harlem Renaissance, called the "New Negro"—a rebellious, progressive-thinking individual who refused to settle for anything less than full social equality. The Renaissance writers spoke in a bold, unrestrained fashion about the inner life and experiences of black Americans, and they were not hesitant to write about the violence, sexuality, and vice that figured prominently in the underclass of black society.

Johnson watched the developments in Harlem with interest and strongly encouraged the younger black writers in their quest for freedom of expression. His novel, *The Autobiography of an Ex-Colored Man*, had influenced many of these younger artists. The

Johnson and his brother, Rosamond (shown here), published two collections of black spirituals in the mid-1920s. Johnson felt that spirituals were the finest expression of black religion and art.

subject of a light-skinned black trying to pass as a white was especially relevant to writers who were rebelling against white society at the same time that they were depending on white patrons and white readers to support their creative work.

Johnson called attention to many outstanding young black writers in his columns in the *New York Age*. In 1922, he brought them further notice when he published *The Book of American Negro Poetry*, an anthology of poems by 40 talented black writers, beginning with Paul Laurence Dunbar and ending with Claude McKay. In his introduction to the book, Johnson traced the history of black poetry from its early writers, such as the 18th-century poet Phillis Wheatley, to its dialect poets, such as Dunbar. He stated that the artistic achievements of black Americans had been limited because "the Negro in the United States is consuming all of his intellectual energy in this grueling race struggle." However, he was sure that cultural experiences shared by white and black Americans would help to soften the attitudes that gave rise to racial prejudice and would allow black artists to achieve a prominent place in American society.

Johnson's childhood encounter with spirituals also fostered a love of black folk music. In 1925, he and Rosamond collaborated on the publication of *The Book of American Negro Spirituals*, a selection of 61 spirituals reproduced in original dialect verse. Rosamond arranged the music, and Johnson wrote a long preface to the book in which he examined the history of spirituals. The brothers published a companion volume, *The Second Book of American Negro Spirituals*, in 1926.

Writing that the spiritual is an art form developed exclusively by black Americans during their centuries of slavery, Johnson stated that these "weirdly sweet" and "wonderfully strong" songs were among the most important contributions that blacks had made to America. In his preface, he described how the influences of African rhythms, slave life, biblical teachings, and black dialect speech had led to the creation of spirituals. In the period following the Civil War, many educated blacks had looked down on spirituals, feeling that the songs were an unwelcome reminder of the hardships of slavery. Johnson's writings helped to renew public interest in spirituals and convinced many people that the songs should be viewed as a treasured musical heritage.

After reading Walt Whitman's poetry collection *Leaves of Grass,* Johnson grew dissatisfied with his own dialect poetry and began to search for a new form of poetic expression. In 1918, while traveling on a recruiting tour for the NAACP, he had heard a black country preacher give a sermon about the creation of the world. Johnson had been struck by the skill with which the preacher recited his story, his voice changing from a whisper to a thunderclap as he swept his audience into a religious frenzy. His speech ultimately inspired Johnson to write a powerful sermon poem, "The Creation." Initially published in 1920, the poem echoes the rhythmic cadence of a preacher's voice, and its colorful imagery and repetitive tones evoke the feeling of the sermons Johnson had heard as a child. The biblical stories that had been passed down from generation to generation became the material for six more sermon poems by Johnson, including "The Crucifixion," "Go Down Death," and "The Judgment Day." In 1927, he published all seven poems in a collection entitled *God's Trombones.*

Johnson hoped that *God's Trombones* would make readers recognize the critical role that preachers played in black American history. These traveling ministers had helped to unite people from a wide variety of Afro-American cultures and had given spiritual strength to millions of oppressed blacks. They had made their style of moral sermonizing and storytelling into a highly imaginative and deeply moving art form.

Along with his sermon poems, Johnson occa-

A respected figure among the artists of the Harlem Renaissance, Johnson brought many younger writers to the attention of the public with The Book of American Negro Poetry, *a collection of works by modern black poets whom he admired.*

sionally wrote poetry that commented directly on racial issues. In 1930, he published "Saint Peter Relates an Incident of the Resurrection Day," a satirical poem that describes the humiliation of white Americans who discover on the Christian Day of Judgment that the unknown soldier in the tomb at Arlington National Cemetery is black. The poem was written in response to the army's treatment of the mothers of black soldiers killed in France during World War I, who were provided with inferior accommodations on army-sponsored trips to the French battleground cemeteries.

After Johnson was awarded the Rosenwald fellowship in 1929, his ensuing study of the black cultural atmosphere in New York led to the publication of *Black Manhattan* in 1930. The book gave a detailed overview of the forces that led to the Harlem Renaissance and paid tribute to the many artists who had helped to win a prominent place for black culture. It focused on the cultural glories of Harlem—its cabarets and stimulating nightlife—rather than on its harsher side, which was filled with poverty, disease, and despair.

Although Johnson concentrated on the positive aspects of Harlem in *Black Manhattan*, his work as a civil rights leader had made him familiar with "the Harlem of doubly handicapped black masses engaged in the grim, daily struggle for existence in the midst of this whirlpool of white civilization." He believed that the lives of the hard-pressed black workers offered artists the opportunity to discover "real comedy and real tragedy, real triumphs and real defeats." According to Johnson, art could be used as a means for increasing understanding between the races and promoting greater social equality.

However, the Harlem Renaissance did not prove to be the overall solution to the racial problems facing black Americans. "The ordinary Negroes hadn't heard

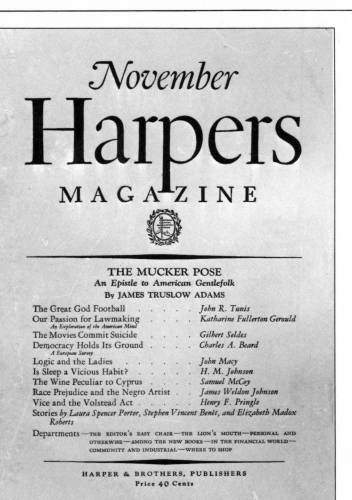

Johnson wrote numerous pieces about the place of black artists in American society, including this article published in Harper's magazine. In 1930, he published Black Manhattan, *a book about the forces behind the Harlem Renaissance.*

of the Negro Renaissance," Langston Hughes said. "And if they had, it hadn't raised their wages any." The recognition given to black writers sometimes encouraged other blacks to think that the color line had disappeared, Du Bois noted. It prompted them to say to themselves, "Keep quiet! Don't complain! Work! All will be well!" Yet this wish did not come true.

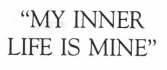

8

"MY INNER
LIFE IS MINE"

W HEN JOHNSON ASSUMED his teaching
position at Fisk University at the end of 1931, he
was able to look back on his 14 years of service in
the NAACP with pride. However, he had been worn
out by both the constant struggle to win funding for
the NAACP and by the competition with other
groups—such as Marcus Garvey's Universal Negro
Improvement Association and the Communist party—
for support within the black community. He wrote
of his experiences, "Not all of the stress and strain
that I experienced while executive head of the Association resulted from efforts to deal with the outside
forces antagonistic to the Negro race; much of it came
from endeavors to rouse Negroes themselves from
apathy, to win over hostile factions. . . . It would be
wrong to think that the Negroes marched as one
united and zealous band under the banner of the
Association."

After Johnson resigned as the head of the NAACP,
he continued to serve the organization in an advisory
role on its board of directors. He also became a vice-
president of the organization. When the global economic structure collapsed in 1929, causing millions
of workers to lose their jobs during the Great Depression, black Americans were especially devastated by

*Johnson became an English professor at Fisk University in 1931,
teaching literature courses during the winter and spring semesters.*

Johnson and Grace stand in front of their cottage at Five Acres, their estate in Great Barrington, Massachusetts, where they often spent their summers.

the hard times. Johnson continued his call for a united front of black groups—led by the NAACP—to press for racial equality during these hard times.

Shortly after the 61-year-old Johnson took up his position as the holder of the Adam K. Spence Chair of Creative Literature at Fisk University, he settled into the pleasant, stimulating routine of life at the Tennessee college. His colleagues included Horace Mann Bond and E. Franklin Frazier—noted experts on black history and culture. The 500 members of the student body made up an enthusiastic group. He taught them courses on American literature, featuring the work of well-known white writers such as Thomas Wolfe and black writers such as his old friend Paul Laurence Dunbar. Johnson's lectures discussed the place of blacks in literature and examined the elements of black culture that had led to the Harlem Renaissance. He taught only during the winter and spring terms, leaving himself plenty of time to write.

In 1933, Johnson published his autobiography,

Along This Way. Most reviewers greeted the book with a favorable notice. Carl Van Doren, a friend and literary critic, described it as "a book any man would have been proud to have written about a life any man would have been proud to have lived."

In his autobiography, Johnson spoke of the need for blacks to maintain a little distance between themselves and the rest of society. He wrote, "If I could have my wish, the Negro would retain his racial identity, with unhampered freedom to develop his own qualities." However, he realized that in the process of integrating more fully into American society, blacks would lose some of their racial consciousness.

At the end of *Along This Way*, Johnson addressed the question of the fate of the black race in the United States. He saw reason for some optimism that the racial situation would steadily improve. Convinced that natural and inevitable forces would help blacks become part of "the American race of the future," he predicted that the black man "will fuse his qualities with those of other groups in the making of the ultimate American people; and that he will add a tint

This intimate photograph of Johnson and Grace was taken by Carl Van Vechten, a writer and critic who befriended many artists of the Harlem Renaissance.

When black Americans were especially hard hit by a worldwide economic depression in the 1930s, the victories of the black heavyweight boxing champion Joe Louis helped to boost their morale. Harlemites are shown here celebrating his victory over Max Baer in September 1935.

to America's complexion and put a perceptible permanent wave in America's hair." If this assimilation did not occur, Johnson concluded, blacks would have no recourse but to isolate themselves and engage in a campaign of fanatical antiwhite hostility that would severely damage American society.

Johnson was not bound to the Fisk campus during his years as a professor. He often made tours of other universities to give lectures on black culture, and he also spoke at conferences of civil rights and business groups. However, the traveling soon put a strain on his physical condition. In 1934, he had to undergo surgery to have an abscess removed from his throat.

After Johnson recovered from the operation, he felt strong enough to take on extra teaching duties. He served as a visiting lecturer on black literature at New York University during the fall semester. From 1934 to 1937, he and his wife lived in their Harlem apartment in the fall, at Fisk University in the winter and spring, and at their house in Great Barrington during the summer.

As time wore on, Johnson had no desire to return to a political or administrative position. He turned down offers to become the consul to Haiti and the president of Atlanta University, which had merged with Spelman and Morehouse colleges. At this point in his life, he preferred to use his wide background on black affairs to write about racial topics.

In 1934, Johnson published an examination of the racial situation in the United States, which he entitled *Negro Americans, What Now?* He wrote the book in response to a series of controversial editorials printed in *The Crisis*, in which Du Bois called for a racially segregated economy. Johnson and the other members of the NAACP board were upset by the editorials. Although Johnson sympathized with Du Bois's frustration over the lack of progress in racial labor problems and agreed that blacks should strive to build their own businesses, he refused to support a philosophy that accepted any form of segregation. He acknowledged the feelings that prompted Du Bois's segregationist statements by saying, "There come times when the most persistent integrationist becomes an isolationist, when he oversees the White world and consigns it to hell." However, he disagreed with the route that Du Bois was proposing that black Americans should take. Winning racial equality *within* American society was the key to black progress, Johnson thought.

In *Negro Americans, What Now?* Johnson stated that although he favored integration, he hoped that

Johnson's book Negro Americans, What Now? *was written in response to the call by W. E. B. Du Bois (shown here) for blacks to separate themselves from the white-controlled business establishment.*

Johnson said of his wife, Grace: "Her sensitive response to what she saw was enchanting. . . . Her delicate patrician beauty stirred something in me."

the achievements of the black race in the United States would eventually win greater recognition. He reviewed problems that were specific to the black race, such as those facing black businessmen hampered by a lack of experience and inability to obtain credit, and examined racial stereotypes that were used to limit opportunities for black Americans. In addition, he again called for a united racial coalition that would be better able to win for blacks the civil rights guarantees and housing, health, and employment benefits to which they were entitled. He termed the coalition a racial "super-power" that would be able to propel blacks from "protest to action . . . to translate declarations into deeds." The struggle for civil rights, he said, was "a campaign that will demand courage, determination and patience . . . the patience to keep on working and fighting."

Johnson concluded *Negro Americans, What Now?* with the warning that blacks should not blame racial prejudice for all their difficulties; problems such as poverty and disease are common to all mankind. The book ends with Johnson's credo:

> I will not allow one prejudiced person or one million or one hundred million to blight my life. I will not let prejudice or any of its attendant humiliations and injustices bear me down to spiritual defeat. My inner life is mine, and I shall defend and maintain its integrity against all the powers of hell.

After a lifetime's struggle against racial oppression and violence, Johnson died suddenly on June 26, 1938—9 days after his 67th birthday. He and his wife had been visiting a friend in Maine, and on their return home to Great Barrington they encountered a heavy rainstorm. Their car was rammed by a speeding train at an unguarded railroad crossing in Wiscasset, Maine. Johnson was killed instantly, and Grace, who had been driving, was badly injured and had to be hospitalized for many weeks.

In Johnson's autobiography, Along This Way, *he stated his optimistic belief that the black man "will fuse his qualities with those of other groups in the making of the ultimate American people."*

Johnson's brother, Rosamond; Rosamond's wife, Nora (right); and Rosamond's daughter Mildred (center) leave Johnson's funeral service in Harlem. Thousands of people from many different backgrounds attended the funeral, anxious to pay tribute to the man who fought so valiantly for racial understanding.

The tributes to Johnson began immediately. Walter White said of him: "With superb and unremitting skill he fought valiantly not only against the lynching, disfranchisement and proscription of his own people, but he fought also to save those who practiced oppression." One of the more poignant statements about Johnson came from an unnamed admirer, who said, "Mr. Johnson climbed very high and he lifted us with him." His funeral service was held at the Salem Methodist Church in Harlem and was attended by thousands of mourners representing the many different groups in American society with which he had been associated.

During Johnson's life of service to the cause of racial equality, he worked in a number of different ways to inspire people with his vision of an America that respects the rights of all its citizens. He was variously employed as an educator, a songwriter, a poet, a novelist, a journalist, a diplomat, and a civil rights leader. While he was involved in each of these occupations, he called for "equal partnership" between the races. But nowhere did he speak more eloquently of liberty, freedom, courage, and human dignity than in the verses of his poems and songs.

Today, many people still find heart in the words penned by Johnson in his song "Lift Every Voice and Sing":

Sing a song full of the faith that the dark past has taught us.
Sing a song full of the hope that the present has brought us.
Facing the rising sun of our new day begun,
Let us march on till victory is won.

The march for human rights continues along the trail that James Weldon Johnson helped so notably to blaze. ❧

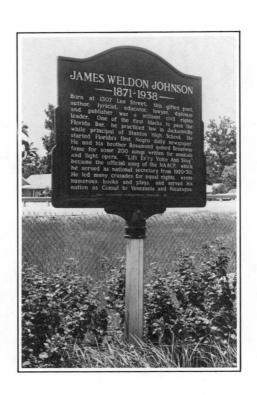

CHRONOLOGY

————— ❦ —————

June 17, 1871	Born James William Johnson in Jacksonville, Florida
1887	Graduates from Stanton School
1894	Graduates from Atlanta University; becomes principal of Stanton School
1897	Becomes the first black to be admitted to the bar in Duval County, Florida
1900	Writes "Lift Every Voice and Sing" with his brother, Rosamond
1901	Forms the songwriting team of Cole and Johnson Brothers in New York City
1902	Resigns from Stanton School; studies dramatic literature at Columbia University
1906	Becomes U.S. consul to Venezuela
1909	Becomes U.S. consul to Nicaragua
1910	Marries Grace Nail
1912	*The Autobiography of an Ex-Colored Man* is published
1914	Johnson becomes editorial writer for the *New York Age*
1916	Becomes field secretary of the NAACP
1920	Becomes executive secretary of the NAACP
1922	*The Book of American Negro Poetry* is published
1925	*The Book of American Negro Spirituals* is published; Johnson receives the Spingarn Award
1927	*God's Trombones* is published
1930	Johnson receives a Julius Rosenwald Fellowship; *Black Manhattan* is published
1931	Becomes a professor at Fisk University
1933	*Along This Way* is published
1934	*American Negroes, What Now?* is published
June 26, 1938	Johnson dies in Maine

FURTHER READING

Johnson, James Weldon. *Along This Way*. New York: Viking, 1933.

———. *The Autobiography of an Ex-Colored Man*. New York: Knopf, 1937.

———. *Black Manhattan*. New York: Atheneum, 1968.

———. *The Book of American Negro Poetry*. New York: Harcourt, Brace and World, 1931.

———. *The Book of American Negro Spirituals*. New York: Viking, 1928.

———. *God's Trombones*. New York: Viking, 1927.

———. *Negro Americans, What Now?* New York: AMS Press, 1971.

———. *Saint Peter Relates an Incident*. New York: Viking, 1935.

Levy, Eugene. *James Weldon Johnson: Black Leader, Black Voice*. Chicago: University of Chicago Press, 1973.

INDEX

PICTURE CREDITS

JANE TOLBERT-ROUCHALEAU was born in Danville, Virginia, and now lives in Gainesville, Florida. She is a graduate of the University of Florida, where she earned a B.A. degree in French and an M.A. degree in journalism and communications. As part of her master's thesis, she traveled "On the Road" with Charles Kuralt. She has two children.

NATHAN IRVIN HUGGINS is W.E.B. Du Bois Professor of History and Director of the W.E.B. Du Bois Institute for Afro-American Research at Harvard University. He previously taught at Columbia University. Professor Huggins is the author of numerous books, including *Black Odyssey: The Afro-American Ordeal in Slavery*, *The Harlem Renaissance*, and *Slave and Citizen: The Life of Frederick Douglass*.